The Stoning of Soraya M.

The Stoning of Soraya M.

Freidoune Sahebjam

Translated from the French
by Richard Seaver

Arcade Publishing · New York

First English-language Edition

Library of Congress Cataloging-in-Publication Data

Sahebjam, Freidoune.
    [Femme lapidée. English]
    The stoning of Soraya M. / Freidoune Sahebjam : translated from the French by Richard Seaver. — 1st English-language ed.
        p. cm.
    ISBN 1-55970-233-8
    1. Adultery — Iran — Case studies. 2. Stoning — Iran — Case studies.   3. Adultery (Islamic law) I. Title.
    HQ806.S2413 1994
    306.73′6′0955 — dc20   93-2173

Published in the United States by Arcade Publishing, Inc., New York

Distributed by Little, Brown and Company

10 9 8 7 6 5 4 3 2 1

BP

Printed in the United States of America

To Safinaz,

To Caroline and Cécile,

To Michèle, who insisted that I bring back this story and who is
no longer here to read it.

Preface

This book relates, in full detail, a case of death by stoning — only one of more than a thousand such cases that
have occurred in Iran over the past fifteen years. After
the shah was deposed and the fundamentalist regime
headed by Ayatollah Khomeini came to power in February 1979, many dubious elements of the population,
including common-law criminals who had been jailed for
good reason under the shah, were released from the
country's prisons. Taking advantage of the religious fervor sweeping the land, a number of these people, especially those with at least a basic knowledge of the
Koran and its tenets, donned clerics' garb, gave themselves the title of mullah, and roamed the country seek-
ing opportunities for self-enrichment or, quite simply,
to conceal their past from the authorities. One such
person was Sheik Hassan in the present work, who was
instrumental in the machinations that resulted in Soraya's death.

Let me backtrack a bit and explain how I chanced
upon the story you are about to read.

Iranian by background, I was born in France, and
grew up partly there and partly in Switzerland, where
my father was a member of the Iranian delegation to
the League of Nations. It was not until I was twenty
years old that I went to my native land, where I

remained for four years, completing my military service. Afterwards, I taught French at the Franco-Iranian Institute in Teheran and English at the Iran America Society. I was a diplomat from 1958 to 1966, and then became a journalist and writer for both French and Iranian magazines and newspapers. Although my family and I knew the shah and the members of the imperial household, I wrote a number of pieces during the 1970s that were critical of the shah, especially in the area of human rights. In fact, my articles earned me the enmity of Savak, the shah's secret political police, which brooked no criticism of state policy and practices.

Late in 1978, a few months before Khomeini 'came to power, I wrote an article for the French newspaper *Le Monde* entitled "Neither Marx Nor Mohammad," in which I warned my compatriots against potential dangers from two quarters. On the one hand, I reminded them of Russia's long-standing desire — dating from before communism, in fact from the turn of the century — to gain not only influence but a solid foothold in a country that could provide it with access to the southern seas, in particular the Persian Gulf. On the other hand, I warned of the efforts of the Shiite clergy to destabilize the pro-Western monarchy of the shah and institute in its place a religious and secretive regime.

On Saturday, May 12, 1979, as I left my apartment building in the Neuilly section of Paris, on my way to visit some friends, a car pulled up to the curb. Four men jumped out, shoved me into the backseat, bound and gagged me, then knocked me out with chloroform. When I woke up I found myself in the basement of a building — which I later learned was the Italian Pavilion of the Cité Universitaire — surrounded by an angry crowd of one hundred bearded and shaggy-haired Iranian students, all of whom were shouting at the top of their lungs and making threatening gestures in my direction. I was tied to a chair in the middle of the room, facing a table on which microphones and recording devices had been set up. I was the first Paris-based victim of an "Islamic trial" similar to those that had been taking place by the hundreds in Iran itself since the return of Khomeini in February of that year. These "trials" inevitably concluded, a few hours later, with the defendant being led out into the courtyard of some prison or military barracks and summarily executed by a firing squad. Some eight hundred ministers, members of Parliament, intimates of the former court, military personnel, intellectuals, and scientists had thus been done away with over the past hundred days. In addition, a list of public enemies, all slated for liquidation, had been drawn up, including members of the royal family, former ministers, army generals, and anyone openly opposed to the new regime. As a mere journalist, I was not on that list, although the previous January I had interviewed the shah just before he was deposed, then done follow-up interviews with him in both Egypt and Morocco. In fact, I was the first journalist to interview him in his early exile, and my articles were picked up by some twenty newspapers and magazines in a number of countries. As a result, I was invited to participate in several radio and television political talk shows to discuss the rapidly evolving situation in Iran, which I did, to the growing irritation of the Iranian embassy in Paris. These, plus my article in *Le Monde,* were doubtless responsible for my kidnapping that Saturday in May.

For eight hours my "trial" went on without interruption: interrogations and blows succeeded each other at an ever-accelerating pace. I was accused of all manner of things: of being a spy, a double agent, an agent provocateur, even a member of the Savak's torture squad. When, finally, word leaked out that something rotten was going on in the basement of the Italian Pavilion, the French police arrived and set me free. I had a broken skull, and eight of my teeth had been knocked out. For eight long hours I had refused to admit my guilt, to mouth my self-criticism, as I had refused to insult the shah or sing the praises of Khomeini.

For the next several days, news of my kidnapping and torture made front-page headlines not only in France but also in Germany, Switzerland, England, and Italy. The immediate effect of the experience was to convince me that in the future I would focus my writing more on politics than I had in the past. Meanwhile, I had to contend with the new realities of my existence. Now condemned to death by Teheran for having "waged war against God" and for "blasphemy against Khomeini," I had to go underground, separate myself from my family, and assume a new identity for the next four years. Only in 1983, when I openly attacked certain members of the opposition for spending most of their time pointlessly fighting one another, did my pursuers begin to relax their vigil. Before long, I apparently became in the eyes of Teheran and its outposts a forgotten person. By then

I had also become a man without nationality, a political refugee, a person deprived of his identity.

Yet even before Teheran had called off its hounds, I had made two trips back to Iran, equipped with false papers, the first in 1981, the second a year later, to see with my own eyes what was really going on. Thus it was that on that second trip, in 1982, I became the first journalist to discover that Khomeini was recruiting and sending into battle against Iraq twelve- to fourteen-year-old boys, some of whom I later met and interviewed in Iraqi POW camps where they lay wounded and dying. From that trip came a book entitled *No More Tears to Cry,* the story of fourteen-year-old Reza, who had been sold by his mother to the Iranian army so that he could sacrifice his life to God and Khomeini. Over the next decade I made seven more trips, always on journalistic assignments, to cover specific stories about the Iranian situation. Twice I was arrested. I could have, and probably should have, been executed both times. But both times I was able to talk — and bribe — my way to freedom. In Iran, everything has its price, if you know how to deal and bargain and have the wherewithal to back up your words with hard currency.

One of those trips was in the fall of 1986, when the French weekly *Paris Match* sent me to investigate the listening stations and satellite dishes that had been set up all along Iran's southeast frontier, where it bordered both Pakistan and Afghanistan. These "spy stations" had been provided by the Russians and were being manned by East German and Bulgarian technicians. At the same time the Chinese and North Koreans were

busy building the secret naval base of Chahbahar in the
deep waters of the the Gulf of Oman. After completing
my assignment, I arrived in a small village not far from
the Pakistan frontier, where I was to await the local
guides who were slated to escort me discreetly back
across the border. I was a few hours ahead of schedule
and was killing time in the little mountain village, trying
to look as inconspicuous as possible. Although I was
dressed in proper Iranian garb, it was clear I was not
a local. Before long an elderly woman, who had been
sitting in her garden, beckoned me to come over and
offered me some tea. That woman was the Zahra
Khanum of this book. I have called the village Kupayeh,
a generic name, for I have preferred to keep the exact
name and location of the real village to myself.

After several glasses of tea, Zahra told me that she
was the aunt of a thirty-five-year-old woman whose
name was Soraya. Had I been in Kupayeh only two
weeks before, the old woman told me, I would have
witnessed a terrible event: Soraya had been stoned to
death for having been unfaithful to her husband. As she
was describing the event to me, she began to tremble
more and more uncontrollably. The worst thing, she
said, was that Soraya was completely innocent. I asked
her how it had happened, what chain of events had
provoked such a terrible crime.

Zahra began to fill me in on the details when my guides
arrived. But the woman was so sincere and convinc-
ing — and I was so intrigued — that before I departed
I promised to return. In fact, I set a precise date to
meet her again, two days after the Iranian New Year,
that is, March 23, 1987.

PREFACE

I came back to the village on the given date. Zahra passed me off as her nephew who lived in a distant part of the country and was spending his vacation with her. During the time I was with her she told me the full story of Soraya, taking me from her niece's childhood up through the terrible day when the "trial" and execution had taken place. Kupayeh was a tiny town of 250 souls, one of a thousand such villages that dot Iran from one end to the other. It is surrounded by meadows and forests and blessed with a clear mountain stream. Through Zahra I met most of the actors in the drama: Soraya's father, her husband, the mayor of the village, Soraya's children and neighbors. I was also able to steep myself in the atmosphere of the town, and Zahra provided me with all the answers I needed to reconstruct the story fairly and accurately. The only person I did not see was the mullah, Sheik Hassan, who was away. Now, barely six months after the event, the villagers — seemingly hardworking and decent folk — appeared to have forgotten their collective crime. After all, stoning had been resurrected and encouraged by the regime of the ayatollahs, and in performing that rite they had only been doing their duty, cleansing their village as hundreds of other villages had been cleansed in years past, "in the name of God the compassionate, the merciful."

When I left Zahra at the end of March I knew that I would never see her again. Marked and broken by that tragedy, she was letting herself drift toward death. She died two years later, although I did not learn of her death until much later, when I was back in Europe.

· · ·

Officially, stoning is prohibited in the territories of Islam, but any religious authority who so desires can suggest that it be done. When a Muslim makes the pilgrimage to Mecca, on the last day of his voyage he passes by Mount Arafat, where stand three gigantic columns that incarnate Satan. At that point the pilgrim takes a stone and casts it symbolically at these columns, as a sign of purification. A woman who betrays her husband is satanic and therefore must be stoned. To be sure, these manifestations of ancient customs never take place in major cities, where the victims are hanged. Stonings occur in the more remote areas of the country and in the mountains, far from prying eyes. Afterward, the villagers boast of what they have done and receive the blessings of the highest religious authorities for "their magnificent act." In the cities, women accused of infidelity can often atone for their sin by paying off a cleric. Thus if they are richer than their husbands, absolution is possible. But in most cases the woman is poor — which means she is a virtual slave to her husband. She has no rights, except for the meager right to remain silent. All the husband needs to win his case of infidelity is two eyewitnesses, who are generally friends and accomplices. As for the accused woman, she has to prove her innocence and that is impossible: no one will come to her aid; no one will bear witness on her behalf.

For all the obvious reasons, hard statistics on the matter of death by stoning are difficult to come by. Yet for the first five years following the installation of the Khomeini regime, that is, from 1979 to 1983, the government acknowledged or proclaimed — depending on one's viewpoint — that between five hundred and six hundred women had thus been put to death. Pulling together further information on the subject from other reliable sources, including the Commission on Human Rights of the UN, Amnesty International, the Red Cross, the Human Rights League, and various Iranian women's groups, one can safely say that at least a thousand women have met their death by stoning in Iran over the past fifteen years. One of the most recent known cases was a stoning that took place in December 1992, in the little town of Karaj, about twenty-five miles from Teheran.

Today, with a view toward improving its image abroad, Iran no longer boasts of its hangings, its stonings, its summary executions. But the hard, sad fact remains that in many parts of the land these barbaric practices are still going on, for the greater glory of an implacable, hard-line, reactionary Islam.

— F. S.

Don't act like the hypocrite
who thinks he can conceal his wiles
by loudly quoting the Koran.

Hafez

1

In SOUTHWESTERN IRAN, roughly thirty-five miles from the city of Kerman, lies the village of Kupayeh — whose name means "at the foot of the mountain." Clinging to the base of austere mountains, the village is a little cluster of brick houses with thatched roofs. It is flanked on one side by an icy, rushing stream and, on the other, by a forest of beech, birch, and olive trees. Beyond stretch fields and meadows, dotted with a few grazing cows and sheep.

Kupayeh is not easily accessible. To get there, you have to take the only road, which is not blacktop; a road that zigzags upward, making several dozen hairpin turns that are as dusty as they are dangerous. Once a week, on market day, a battered old bus swings and sways up the road and arrives at Kupayeh in the morning. It brings a number of passengers, most of them peasants, whose merchandise is piled on top of the bus. They come to sell these wares or exchange them for other goods, which they will take back down to the valley and try to sell there.

It was in the village of Kupayeh that Soraya was born in 1951.

She had come into the world on the Shah's wedding day and had been named after his bride, Princess

Soraya. The whole country was celebrating the happy occasion.

Morteza Ramazani, who had married rather late in life, was duly proud of this gift from God. "She will be the most beautiful girl in the village," he announced. "And I shall give her in marriage to the best young man in town. He will have to prove himself worthy."

Shokat, the child's mother, was a pious woman of fragile health. She had had her first child when she was thirteen and subsequently gave birth to four more children, two of whom died in infancy. After Soraya was born, a doctor came from Kerman to examine Shokat. He informed Morteza in no uncertain terms that another pregnancy might well prove fatal.

Whereupon Morteza took a *sigheh,* * as the law stipulated, a second wife, who moved into the house and bore him four more children.

All lived together in harmony, but Shokat remained the preferred woman of the house. The concubine was assigned all the lowliest tasks and chores, which she carried out for many years without the slightest complaint. When Shokat's illness paralyzed her, the two eldest sons and Soraya assumed responsibility for running the household. All three also had the advantage of knowing how to read and write, so they could read the Koran and the local posters to other members of the family. They had learned these skills at the village

---

*A glossary of italicized words which cannot be fairly or properly translated, because of their local meaning or connotation, can be found at the back of the book.

school. The village school did not open every day, for the schoolmaster was also the town potter, and when he had to oversee the firing of his pots, the children were free to play in the fields. It was on one of these school holidays that Soraya had her first encounter with Ghorban-Ali. She was five years old at the time, and he was a boy of twelve.

Ghorban-Ali had decided to make a kite. He had spent hours on end gluing together bits of wood and pieces of paper of many colors, but try as he might, the kite just wouldn't fly. Either the wood would be too heavy, or the paper would rip under the force of the wind, or the glue wouldn't stick, or the string would break. Eventually, Ghorban-Ali got the kite to fly. The great moment had finally arrived. Twenty or so children, ranging in age from five to fifteen, gathered in the meadow. They all held their breath, and the kite rose slowly and majestically heavenward. It was an occasion of great festivity. One by one, the children were each given the chance to fly the kite themselves. Now it was Soraya's turn. Shyly, she ran across the meadow, the kite at the end of the long string. As she watched the crowd that was cheering her on, she stumbled on a stone and fell down. She let go of the kite, which soared high into the sky, then fell back toward the ground. When Soraya, whose knee was scratched and bleeding, painfully pulled herself to her feet, her little comrades had disappeared. . . .

She ran all the way home and hid there.

Her mother bandaged her knee, and before long she went back outdoors. She had taken only a few steps when the children, all out of breath, began to scold and upbraid her: "Come and see what you've done. . . . You're a dumbbell! We never want you to play with us again!"

The child had no idea how to defend herself.

"Come on," Ghorban-Ali shouted at her, "come over here and see where you made the kite land."

He grabbed the little girl by the wrist and dragged her toward the lower end of the village, the other children all following in their wake. The kite was perched atop a beech tree, so high up there was no way to get it down. The biggest ladder in Kupayeh was no higher than thirteen feet, and none of the poles they used to beat the trees when they picked nuts was long enough, either. It was impossible to climb the tree; its branches were much too frail to sustain the weight of even an adolescent. As for hugging and shaking the tree, how could they even consider that as a possible solution when its trunk was far too big around for a child to get a good grasp.

"You'll have to build us another kite. And until you do, you can't play with us any more."

Thus did Ghorban-Ali proclaim his decision. It was seconded by all the other children, who threw handfuls of sand and gravel at Soraya. In response, she scrunched down her head as far as she could, and waited. Although she was sad and upset, she didn't want to cry in front of her friends. She repressed a sob and closed her eyes tight. Then, when she could no longer hear any sound around her, she raised her head and saw that only her cousin Massoumeh had remained behind, sitting beside her.

"Don't worry," Massoumeh said. "I'll help you make

another one. Wait and see, it'll be even more beautiful than that one."

"I hate Ghorban-Ali, I hate him, I hate him. I never want to see him again as long as I live." After this incident, Soraya's life was uneventful for several years.

When she was ten, her parents took her down to the city to complete her education by becoming an apprentice at the home of the *arbab*, the wealthy landowner.

The children who apprenticed there were given food and lodging, but they received no salary. They worked fifteen hours a day and slept little, since even at night they were often awakened on one pretext or another.

The little girl did not like the arbab, this fat, unkempt, and arrogant man who frequently beat her. But what could you do when you were dealing with a man as powerful as he was, a man who always kept a gun in his car? She bowed her head, asked his forgiveness, and kissed the master's hand. For three years she had to endure all the humiliations and vexations of an angry man and put up with his advances as soon as his wife was away. Each time it was the same. He summoned the girl to his room, undressed her slowly, said things to her she didn't understand, and, when she was naked, he kissed her budding breasts as he masturbated. The child understood nothing, felt nothing, said nothing. As thanks, he would offer her some pistachios or dates, and at dawn she was back at work.

For three years she did not see her parents, but sometimes one of her brothers would come to pay her a visit. She was allowed to spend a quarter of an hour with him in the garden.

It was imperative for Soraya to remain a virgin until she was married, and the fat man knew it; otherwise the scandal would be so great that the arbab would have to indemnify the child's father. At that time, long before the revolution, the authorities were uncompromising when it came to any kind of sexual debauchery.

The two sons of the landowner poked fun at Soraya, pinched her breast, and let their hands roam over her buttocks, but they went no further, since they knew she belonged to their father. One day one of the boys was roundly slapped when he laid a hand on the girl while his father was in the room. Terrified, Soraya ran out of the room and hid in the cellar.

A week later, she returned home to Kupayeh for good.

By the time she came back to Kupayeh, Soraya was almost a young woman: she was thirteen, and it was decided that she should be given in marriage to Ghorban-Ali, who was twenty, in exchange for several head of cattle, a plot of land, and several rugs.

When Ghorban-Ali saw Soraya again, he didn't recognize her. That day he knew for the first time what it was to feel like a man. He had never had the slightest experience with a woman. First, because there were no suitable women in the village; second, because he had never been to the city; and finally, because even if he had somehow managed to make it to the city, he never had enough money in his pocket to go to a whorehouse in Kerman anyway. While there were plenty of girls in the village, they were either too young, or they had no dowry, or he found them too ugly.

Each time the fat man arrived in the village for one of his periodic visits, the entire community gathered on the town square to welcome the master. He was the man who owned all the houses, all the fields and meadows, and, above all, the water of the rushing stream, and who rented his land to the peasants. The inhabitants came up to him and kissed his hands or feet as a sign of allegiance, then begged the Omnipotent to protect the arbab and his family from illness, divine anger, or any possible misfortune that might befall them. And each villager brought a suitcase, a package, a *samovar*, or provisions of one sort or another to the big house situated a short distance away. That same evening other children were introduced to him.

The marriage of Soraya to Ghorban-Ali took place shortly after his return from Kerman, in the autumn of 1964. For the occasion, a *mullah* came up to the village, as did a company of strolling musicians.

The villagers had dressed in their best finery; the men were all clean-shaven; the women, decked out in glittering jewelry. At dusk a roaring fire was lit on the main square, where the mullah performed the ceremony. The arbab and his family were comfortably ensconced on a profusion of rugs and cushions. At nightfall, the festivities began.

Soraya remained off to one side, surrounded by the women of the village. The most active of the women was without question Soraya's Aunt Zahra, who wanted the ceremony to be perfect. She had shown endless ingenuity in making up the young woman: she had plucked her eyebrows, reddened her lips and cheeks, colored her hair with a touch of henna, put mascara on

7

her eyelashes and kohl around her eyes; she had affixed to her forehead a gold-and-turquoise pendant. Then she had painted Soraya's fingernails, and offered her her most beautiful *chador*, woven of silk and silver, because she wanted her niece to be the most beautiful bride the village had ever seen.

As tradition required, Aunt Zahra covered the young bride's face with a veil, which she wore throughout the ceremony, so that no one would see her before the marriage was consummated.

Meanwhile, the festivities were in full swing. Three sheep had been slaughtered, then smeared with oil and impaled on spits that were now turning slowly above the fire that sent showers of sparks into the night sky. The musicians were playing, and the men, one after another, rose and danced in slow circular movements. The women, off to one side, clapped their hands joyously. The arbab was served his food on plates, but in keeping with the villagers' customs, he ate the lamb and rice with his hands. The singing and dancing lasted late into the night. At the first light of dawn, the fire was extinguished and all the villagers repaired to their houses to sleep. For the last time, the two betrothed slept in their parents' houses. The next day the mullah joined the young couple in marriage in the town hall, in the presence of the *kadkhoda*.

Three times the mullah asked the young man if he wanted to take Soraya to be his wife. Twice, Ghorban-Ali made no response. The third time, he said yes. The same question was asked three times of the young woman. She, too, acquiesced the third time.

They kissed the Koran that was offered to them;

8

they both signed the marriage registry; and the mullah read the marriage act. In addition to the dowry that Soraya brought with her from her parents, the arbab had insisted on offering his former domestic a beautiful samovar, a rug, an oil lamp, and a small amount of money.

As for Ghorban-Ali, aside from a necklace that his mother had given him, a *khorsi* for the long winter evenings, and a worn antique rug, what he essentially brought to the marriage was a commitment to work and to support his wife and his future family.

That evening, under the supervision of Soraya's Aunt Zahra, the women carefully prepared the bride for the marriage night. She was washed, totally depilated, and perfumed. When her husband was alone with her at last, she said nothing to him. He extinguished the only lamp in the house, threw himself upon her, and forcefully penetrated her.

Ten months later Hussein-Ali was born, followed by a stillborn child and, two years later, Hassan-Ali. Next she gave birth to two girls, Maryam and Leila, then another child who was stillborn, and more children. Her last child, little Khojasteh, was born during the year of the revolution. In the space of fourteen years, Soraya gave birth to nine children, including the two who died at birth.

Like his father before him, Ghorban-Ali was naturally lazy, but this did not mean he was not always on the lookout for some dubious projects and easy profits. Anything that was on the fringes of legality interested him. He was a bit of a poacher, and a petty thief whenever the occasion presented itself. It was the Islamic revolution, and the changes it brought about in his village, that gave him the chance to make himself important.

Once a month he took the bus into the city for reasons of business. What business? Soraya never really knew, but each time he came back he had a few hundred *rials* in his pocket, just enough to provide his family with the bare necessities.

Little by little Ghorban-Ali abandoned his wife. In the village, rumor had it that he was having an affair in the city with a divorced woman whose brother was in constant contact with the black marketers of Zahedan. People spoke of precious jewels, of American cigarettes, of alcohol, and even of drugs. The police had come up to the village from Kerman to question first the mayor — the kadkhoda — then Ghorban-Ali, but they had left empty-handed. A man had been killed down in the valley, in the course of some brawl, and Soraya's husband was known to have been in the general vicinity at the time. He was ordered not to show his face in the city again. From then on he became taciturn, more violent, and continually beat his wife and his children. Once Soraya showed up at her mother's house, her face badly bloodied, carrying her youngest child in her arms. For a week she refused to return home. It was Zahra who went over to her house and cooked and cleaned for the angry husband, until finally Ghorban-Ali repented and begged his father-in-law's forgiveness.

The years had taken their toll on Soraya. Her looks had faded. She appeared far older than her twenty-eight years when the old regime fell and the republic was proclaimed. All the portraits of the shah and his wife immediately disappeared. They were replaced by some severe-looking characters with beards and turbaned heads.

In the village, nothing changed, except that the news spread that the new regime had once again authorized men to have several wives. Without wasting a minute, Ghorban-Ali turned his back on his wife and no longer even touched her. She did not complain about the new situation. He showed up at home only rarely, and often disappeared into the valley for three or four days in a row. Soraya, increasingly unobtrusive, became as discreet as a shadow, as if she were ashamed at having been unable to hold on to her husband.

"I want to die," she said to her mother one evening. "I want to die, Mama. I can't bear it any longer. He beats me, he insults me, he beats the children."

Silent, Shokat Khanum didn't know what to say to her daughter, for the village tradition prohibited parents from involving themselves in the affairs of their son-in-law's family. To make matters worse, men's authority had been absolute. For some time now, they alone made all the decisions. And then there were the village gossips who said that if Ghorban-Ali went prowling down to the city so often instead of staying home with his family, it was because Soraya was a bad wife.

Soraya felt ashamed whenever she crossed the village square. People no longer greeted her when she walked by; they spoke to her briefly, if at all; and some of the villagers even went so far as to avoid her. What did they reproach her for? What had she done? They blamed

11

her for not having known how to keep her husband the way the other women in Kupayeh had, for lowering her head instead of holding it high, for having been incapable of settling her problems without always having to call on her parents, for having a thieving and lying son who was forever stirring up trouble in the village. In short, for being a bad wife and an unworthy mother.

Only a few friends sympathized with her, and they did so discreetly, never inviting her into their homes.

Soraya wrapped herself in a cloak of silence, speaking only with her youngest child and with Zahra, crying quietly by herself, not responding in any way whenever her husband or son beat her.

Soon Soraya had another tragedy to bear — the death of her mother. She reacted by locking herself up in her house and refused to cook for a week. She resumed her activities on the seventh day, when her father came to visit her and give her her mother's necklace.

Soraya kissed the necklace, then her father's hands. She accompanied him to the threshold of the house and whispered to him: "Don't forget, Papa, I love you."

Then she closed the door behind him.

One day all the villagers had left Kupayeh in commemoration of *sizda bedar*, as tradition called for. They left their houses far behind, so that a purifying spirit could cleanse them of all the impurities of the past year. Soraya, who had remained in her house, was surprised to hear a door slam. She went to the window. Ghorban-Ali had just emerged from an American-made automobile, together with a woman. The two of them were heading toward the house. She heard the front door

12

open, then close softly. She could hear muffled voices, but the words were barely audible. The couple was laughing, and whatever they were saying they both seemed to be having a good time. Then there was a long silence, the meaning of which Soraya understood. She was overcome with shame. How was it possible that he could bring into her own house, into her own bed, an unknown woman, a whore that you could probably buy for a few hundred rials, while she barely had enough money to buy food for her children?

Half an hour later, they got back into the car and headed down toward the plain.

When Soraya emerged from her hiding place, the house reeked of powder and perfume. As she was straightening up the bedroom, her Aunt Zahra Khanum came in. The two women exchanged looks for a brief moment, then the old woman said simply: "I saw everything. I, too, stayed home today. . . . Don't say a thing. I'm here!"

And the black silhouette disappeared as quickly as she had arrived.

Soraya knew that Ghorban-Ali was in the habit of paying occasional visits to the prostitutes down in Kerman. She knew because when he came home his clothes often smelled of cheap perfume. But never before had he brought one of the creatures into their house; never before had an unknown woman slept in their bed.

Soraya also knew that Ghorban-Ali was involved in some dubious ventures outside the village, for the simple reason that for some time now he had seemed increasingly well off. She knew that the arbab had been arrested. But why was her husband driving the arbab's

13

old American car? And where had he learned to drive? Who had taught him?

Soraya would have a hard time answering these questions for she had severed virtually all relations with the outside world. The only people she allowed to visit her at home were her father; her confidante, Zahra Khanum; and the kadkhoda.

Whenever Ghorban-Ali came back from the city, he became a holy terror in his own home: he lashed out at any member of his family who happened to cross his path, beating anyone who had the misfortune to come within reach of his flailing hand. But there was still no cry or shout from Soraya, for she endured his abuse in silence. If she did cry, it was to herself, and she did her best to hide until the storm blew over.

Only the youngest children cried when their father struck them.

Soraya also noticed that her husband and the new village mullah, Sheik Hassan, often talked together at great length, as though there was a strange complicity between them. To her, it looked as if Ghorban-Ali was fascinated by the culture, the wealth, and the authority of the man of God. He was envious of the man's elegance and the ease with which Sheik Hassan had imposed himself on the village. Ghorban-Ali's efforts to emulate the mullah in one way or another were pitiful. Ghorban-Ali still talked like a boor, a country bumpkin; the clothes he wore were still sloppy and ill-fitting; and he still wore a thick beard. He spent little time at the *hamman*, the public steam baths, and despite the cheap eau de cologne he sprayed on himself, he still smelled. For his part,

14

Sheik Hassan had understood that Ghorban-Ali could be useful to him in a number of ways, and made a special effort to seek him out whenever possible. When he spoke with Ghorban-Ali, he forced himself to adopt another language, a simpler vocabulary, more popular words. Before long, Soraya saw the two men meet, exchange hearty embraces, patting each other stoutly on the back as they hugged, and laugh heartily as they exchanged either bank notes or envelopes.

As for his manner toward Soraya, the mullah was pointedly and insistently courteous. She hated the heavy looks he gave her, and every time he tried to strike up a conversation, she cut him short. Yet one day when she was alone at home, the sheik entered her house unannounced, asked if he could sit down, and began talking to her: "Soraya Khanum, I am here at the request of Ghorban-Ali. . . ."

She had suspected as much; in fact, she had been anticipating this conversation for some time now.

Hassan had taken out his prayer box from his pocket, and having set his Koran on the low table, he went on: "Your husband has come to me to lodge a complaint against you: he says you no longer speak to him, that you neglect him, that, in a sense, you have abandoned him."

Soraya gazed at him, motionless, without lowering her eyes.

"He is your husband. . . . He has all the rights you know very well, all the rights. You cannot refuse him anything. He is a good husband, a good provider who brings money home, a man who loves his children."

The young woman felt like smiling, but she refrained. Still, she could not repress a slight grin, which she was able to conceal behind a corner of her veil.

"Ghorban-Ali would like to come to reach a settlement with you. We have discussed the matter at great length, he and I, and I believe his proposition to be eminently fair. Here is what he would like."

Sheik Hassan cleared his throat, adjusted his spectacles on his nose, furtively ran his hand through his beard, and went on: "He would like a divorce, for he has met another woman in the city whom he would like to marry. But he does not have the means to support two wives. He is, however, prepared to give you the house, the children, the furniture, and the little field that you can cultivate for your own needs. But he will not give you a single rial more."

Hassan raised his eyes toward Soraya and awaited her response, but to no avail. Then he spoke again: "The proposal strikes me as fair. You two separate; I shall draw up the act of divorce; and henceforth neither of you will owe the other party anything. He is leaving you everything. That's more than generous, don't you agree?"

The veiled woman still did not respond.

"Soraya Khanum, we are here alone, just the two of us. I am a man of God; I am like the Prophet; you can confide in me. What do you have to say?"

Hassan shifted uncomfortably, as if he were embarrassed, then continued: "There's also something else I want to propose to you. This comes from me and me alone. Ghorban-Ali has nothing to do with it. Now then, what I want to suggest is, how shall I put it?"

The man, more and more embarrassed, was sweating profusely, his fingers clicking noisily as he shook his prayer box.

"What I am proposing, what I really want to say is that I would be happy to provide both for you and for your charming children. You are so deserving. This would be done with the utmost propriety, of course, completely honorably! I would come to pay you a visit from time to time; we would talk; we would get to know each other better. . . ."

The mullah was so worked up he could not sit still in his chair. Soraya was standing in front of him, frozen.

At that moment, Zahra appeared. She had been in the next room, and Hassan had not seen her. She walked up to the sheik, who, taken completely aback, leaped to his feet.

"Mister Hassan Lajevardi or whoever you really are, leave this house before I go out and stir up the whole village. You should be ashamed of yourself! And may the wrath of God rain down upon you! Creature of the Devil, may the undertaker bear you away, you and yours unto the third generation! . . . Monster!"

For a moment it was obvious the mullah was upset; then he regained control of himself. "But Zahra Khanum, you have misunderstood me. . . . You have mistaken my intentions. . . . I have the utmost respect for Soraya Khanum. . . . What in the world were you thinking?"

"I was thinking that you are a vile, unspeakable person, and that your garb and your turban ought to render you a bit more worthy. You disgrace and dishonor the

Holy Book you are carrying. . . . Leave this house immediately, and never set foot in it again!"

From that day on, Hassan vowed that he would one day get his revenge on the daughter of Morteza Ramazani. But he knew that as long as Zahra was there to support and sustain the young woman, he would have his work cut out for him.

2

I T WAS AFTER the revolution, when its effects were just being felt in the village of Kupayeh, after considerable delay, that Ghorban-Ali began the process of abandoning his wife. He had become friends with the driver of the bus that came up to the village once a week. The driver, whose name was Nasrollah, told Ghorban-Ali what was going on down in the valley. He talked to him about the big city, about its stores and cafes, about his pals, and about the easy women you encountered there. And he talked to him about the money that could be made there.

Fascinated, Ghorban-Ali decided one day to join Nasrollah in his drive back down to the city. At first he went there once a month, riding the bus back up to the village the following week. Then it was every two weeks. He took advantage of the comings and goings of the wheezy old bus, which transported, in addition to a few passengers, poultry, a head of sheep from time to time, fresh fruits and vegetables, and assorted packages. Down at Kerman, Ghorban-Ali sometimes slept at Nasrollah's, or at the bus station, or else in the back of a cafe where he made himself useful by serving tea or *sharbat*.

He discovered in the streets of the city, and in its cafes, an exhilarating and intoxicating universe. He ran errands for this person or that, delivering messages,

19

carrying envelopes and packages, bowing and scraping before the people he deemed important. But his peasant look and language did not allow him to mix with those men he sorely wanted to emulate.

Little by little, his devotion and spontaneity made people like him; he changed completely. He began to use words that had never been heard back up in the mountains, words that only city dwellers knew. He spoke of bank drafts, of loans, of investments. In short, he told anyone who would listen that he was involved in business. The only problem was, no one quite knew what business he was in.

Soraya said nothing. On several occasions he had run-ins with both the local and national police, for the envelopes and packages he carried contained "forbidden merchandise." Machdi Ebrahim, the kadkhoda, would say nothing more than that, but the town quickly understood that Soraya's husband had become a petty trafficker, and among the services he rendered were receiving and concealing stolen goods, and dealing in contraband.

She never questioned him about his activities and indeed never expected him to talk to her about them.

One day the national police drove up to the village in a Jeep. There were three of them, a sergeant and two other soldiers. They spoke to the mayor for a long time, then interrogated Ghorban-Ali and his father, and left town. It was never known exactly what was said, but Soraya knew that, in general, they talked about the people that Ghorban-Ali hung around with down in the city.

After that public affront, Ghorban-Ali became even

harsher and more violent with his family. At the slightest annoyance, he would beat his wife or the child she was holding in her arms. The national police issued a formal warning: he was restricted to the village. "If we find you in the city, you can be sure you'll spend the night in prison."

Once again, Ghorban-Ali spent his days hanging out in the village streets, doing odd jobs here and there for various people, trekking up into the hills with his old buddies, who for the past several months he had forsaken, and waiting for the opportunity to return to the city. He had grown to like city life; he felt at home there, but here within the confines of this tiny village, where nothing ever happened, he felt restricted, suffocated.

In Kerman, he had learned a great deal in a very short time. Going to a cafe, just sitting there and watching the people and the cars go by, fascinated him. Hundreds, even thousands of people passed before his eyes, people he didn't know, people who pushed or shoved him as they rushed about their business; whereas he was content to sit and wait for someone to call or summon him to do some dubious odd job or perform some task that was, more often than not, shady. He was available; people knew where to find him.

The more he expounded to the villagers on his memories of life down in the city, the more he felt that he had to return there as quickly as possible. He even told them about the time when he had done a service for someone, and his payment had been a session with a prostitute. He explained how he had been taken down a quiet little street, at the end of which was a house in

21

which several young prostitutes were waiting for men to service. His employers picked out one for him, and he made love to her savagely, without ever addressing a word to the woman — he never even knew her name. He swore he was going back to the place as soon as he could.

In the wake of the revolution, a lot of people were killed in Kerman and throughout the entire province. Old disputes being settled, local rivalries, rapid executions, betrayals, desertions, cleansings. It was only in the autumn, eight months after the *ayatollah* had come to power in Teheran, that Ghorban-Ali deemed it safe to go back down to Kerman. He got off the bus at the last stop before the city, instead of at the immense square where the Friday Mosque stood, preferring to be discreet.

"Ghorban-Ali! Ghorban-Ali!"

He gave a start, looked across the street, and recognized one of his old drinking companions whose name he couldn't remember.

"Come here! Come on over!"

Ghorban-Ali hesitated for a moment, then crossed the street. The two men greeted each other, exchanged a few amenities, then the city dweller said: "Look. My own shop. I own it outright. In the old days I used to work here for a bastard who was loyal to the shah and who owned several shops in the city. I took part in the revolution and was rewarded by the imam. I'm my own boss. I sell fruits and vegetables, drinks and candies."

Ghorban-Ali was amazed.

"Come on, don't just stand there. Let me offer you

a cup of tea, and we'll talk a little business. I'm sure a guy like you can make himself a pile of money."

Ghorban-Ali spent three days and three nights with his friend — whose name was Mansour — helping him restock the shop, waiting on customers, shouting out the prices of the merchandise to passersby, and, in the evening, helping to tidy up the place.

"Say, did it ever occur to you that you might like to work for the imam?"

"Sure, of course I'd like to, but I don't know anyone around here."

"That's nothing to worry about. I know everyone. My friends and I are going to help you."

Ghorban-Ali was introduced to a neighbor, who in turn introduced him to the assistant of the new police chief of that section of town. Thus, from one day to the next, Ghorban-Ali found himself hired as a guard in the local prison, with a steady salary. He thought he must be dreaming.

Even more amazing, he learned soon after he started his new job that the arbab, who had been arrested a few weeks before, was incarcerated in "his" prison.

Huddled there at the back of his cell, the man was unrecognizable, and to gain his freedom he was prepared to make any sacrifice. The more Ghorban-Ali demanded, the more the hard-pressed fat man was disposed to give. That was all well and good, but it did not solve the one major problem: how to get one's hands on his assets. The ex-landowner was in prison, his goods and possessions were elsewhere.

Ghorban-Ali confided in Mansour, who advised him

to be circumspect. "Let's not be in a hurry," he said. "If we proceed too quickly, people will notice what we're doing. Patience is what's called for here."

The problem was, patience was not among the qualities Soraya's husband possessed. He had always wanted everything right away.

"Your arbab is not an important person," Mansour advised. "He hasn't done anything very serious. There are lots of others in here who will be tried and sentenced before he will, people who have stolen millions, who have starved the people, defrauded half the city. We have dozens in here who fall into that category, and in two other people's prisons as well. Your fellow may be important to you and your friends back in your village, but nobody here in the city gives a damn about him. Let him stew in his own juices here for a while, for as long as it takes. He'll be softened up even more in a few months."

Mansour was right. The trials and executions did indeed follow in rapid succession, and still the arbab's name did not appear on any list. As the weeks went by, the man who had once been fat was wasting away, and his former arrogance disappeared as well. He knew that Ghorban-Ali was his protector, the person who would vouch for him, but he also knew that at any moment he could be dragged from his cell and brought before his judges.

Months later his name did finally appear for the first time on a list of persons suspected of crimes against the people and liable to be sentenced. For a while Mansour and his friend managed to make sure that the paper on which the arbab's name appeared was always lost or misplaced. On one occasion they simply erased his name from the sheet. But they had to move fast, especially after a strange new character had been on the scene for a few weeks, a man who seemed to have considerable influence and authority among the judges, in the prison, and among the people's committees.

He claimed to have come from Teheran, that he personally knew the ayatollah, who had dispatched him to Kerman on a special mission. Everyone called him Mr. Lajevardi, and he further maintained that he was related to one of the leading dignitaries of the regime. In short, he plotted and schemed, and people distrusted him. To insinuate oneself with the man, to become not even a friend but an accomplice, one had to resort to a thousand wiles, one had to flatter the man to death and bow and scrape endlessly before him. Lajevardi was also a friend of the police commissioner in that part of the city, who in turn had a cousin on the people's court. Everyone in this fine, upstanding little group had keys, letterhead stationery, and the necessary official stamps to create false papers. It was child's play to legalize the donations that the arbab made to his jailers, and especially to Ghorban-Ali.

When the day of his trial arrived, the former landowner appeared before his judges without a worry in the world. He had seen that his benefactors were there in the courtroom. But when he heard the sentence pronounced — "In the name of God, you are hereby sentenced to be hanged before sunset today" — he fainted.

The fortune of the late arbab was divided among his acolytes, with Ghorban-Ali receiving the most modest share: the house in the city in which he was living, his parents' house in the village, a plot of land, free access to the water of the village stream, ten thousand rials in cash, and the arbab's automobile. From that moment on, Ghorban-Ali had the feeling that he had really become somebody. He was greeted wherever he went; he was offered tea or clusters of fruit when he walked through the streets of Kerman; people sought out his company.

There were some, however, who made a point of shunning him. To work in the prison as a salaried employee, and sleep there, did not bother Ghorban-Ali, but it did bother certain others. For just as he could help some people, he could, according to his whims and desires, lock up whomever he wanted whenever he wanted.

He still carried on his shady activities, sharing the proceeds with his superiors or, at times, simply robbing them blind. The welcome mat was always out for him at the local whorehouse. In short, in that part of town, in the neighborhood of the Friday Mosque, he had become a well-known figure.

It was only natural, therefore, that when he returned to Kupayeh it was as Mister Somebody, and he talked endlessly about his exploits and business affairs down in the city.

It was about this time that the government decreed that henceforth the villagers would become owners of their own homes. From then on, all the neighboring lands became part of the collective farm; and water was free to one and all.

Up there in the village, Ghorban-Ali let it be known that he was the director of the prison. In fact, he did have in his possession the keys to all the cells and to all the prison offices. Having an intimate acquaintance with the prison seals and official papers, he was even capable of surreptitiously freeing some prisoners, in return for some truly staggering payments in hard cash.

Everyone in the city had at least one relative behind bars and, one day or another, needed the help and services of Ghorban-Ali. He had opened a bank account which soon grew by leaps and bounds. He had rented a large safe deposit box in which he stored various bunches of keys handed over to him by various prisoners, bank drafts, deeds to property, insurance papers, stocks and bonds, jewelry, and much more besides.

And then Ghorban-Ali fell in love.

For the first time in his life he was in love with a woman. And not just any woman. Not a peasant or a shopkeeper, and certainly not one of those girls from the whorehouse whose favors he had enjoyed.

No, the person he had fallen in love with was a girl he had spotted when she had come to the prison to visit her father. She was beautiful beneath her chador, her face very pale, her eyes green, her lips delicate. He was immediately smitten. But how could he approach her? How old could she be? Fourteen, maybe fifteen. She came twice a week, standing in line for hours in the sun in front of the main gate of the prison, with the wives and daughters of those who were incarcerated there.

After quickly making inquiries, Ghorban-Ali learned that her father was a doctor, that prior to the revolution he had had a wide circle of patients among the wealthier people of Kerman, and that he had never concealed his

27

monarchist sentiments. Since he was so well known and respected, the revolutionary authorities had left him alone for a time, since they needed his medical expertise. But one day the order had come down from the capital to arrest the man. Thus it was that Ghorban-Ali made the acquaintance of Mehri.

Every night before he went to bed he thought of her, and he thought of her each time he went to visit the girls at the whorehouse on the Avenue Darvaseh Zahedan. He saw himself holding her in his arms, pictured himself caressing her, talking to her, breathing in her perfume. With a wife like that, he said to himself, wouldn't they almost have to promote me to a more important position, perhaps even make me the prison director?

From that time on, he could never understand how he had been able to spend so many years of his life in Kupayeh. He was even ashamed to admit to his fellow guards that his father was a shepherd. He preferred to tell them that his father was a shopkeeper who also had a herd of sheep. It was true, actually, because following the demise of the arbab and the distribution of his goods and possessions, Ghorban-Ali's father, Lotfollah, had inherited a street stall and a few ewes.

Finally, Ghorban-Ali could no longer bear Soraya. He did not want to live any longer with that silent, resigned woman who was old before her time and, what was worse, completely above reproach.

He had tried to humiliate her by telling his childhood friends about his sexual exploits down in the city; he had tried to make her jealous by telling her about all the cars he had driven; and he had tried to torment her by describing the young women of the city who were beautiful, who dressed elegantly and wore perfumes that smelled like roses. But Soraya said nothing and seemed to hear nothing.

One evening he added: "It's not out of the question that I remarry and have other children. I want them to go to school, to the best schools. There's this one school in Kerman I know about. . . . I think that's where I'd want them to go."

Still no reaction from the young woman, who was darning socks by the light of a single candle.

Hussein-Ali, the eldest son, said: "What does this woman look like, Father? Describe her to us."

Ghorban-Ali glanced over at his wife, who was still bent over her work, and went on, drawing deeply on his water pipe:

"She's young. She's as beautiful as a miniature. She's very well educated. Her father's a doctor. We like each other."

"Have you already talked with her?"

"Many times . . . each time that she visits the prison, in fact. I let her go to the head of the line. The waiting line is just too long. She's extremely grateful."

He was lying, for he had never yet spoken a word to the girl, but he would have gone to any lengths to provoke his wife. He used every wile at his command, every device he could think of, to try to induce her to do or say something he could use against her.

He drove up from the city, bringing with him a city woman, whom he had picked up at the whorehouse and outfitted with a pair of sunglasses. To make sure people noticed him, he drove around the village square three

29

times, pulled up and stopped in front of the fountain, said hello to a few people he knew, then drove off in a great cloud of dust. No one ever commented on his visits; the villagers were all afraid that Ghorban-Ali might indeed have political connections down in the valley that might someday be used against the town. The consensus still was that he was a ne'er-do-well, and they feared him as if he were the plague.

The one who feared this prison guard the most was Sheik Hassan, who had only recently arrived in the village. To him, Ghorban-Ali was volatile and unpredictable and, he was afraid, might turn on him at any moment. These were troubled times; people simply seemed to vanish off the face of the earth. The mullah himself, it was said, had had to make a hasty retreat from Kerman, under conditions that still remained somewhat obscure. He apparently left after a meeting with some Islamic judge, who had never been seen since.

So it was better to be on good terms with Ghorban-Ali.

One winter, Firouzeh, Soraya's childhood girlfriend, died of pneumonia, leaving behind two children and a husband, Hashem. Hashem was a serious, hardworking young man, a blacksmith by trade. He was also Ghorban-Ali's cousin. Like his father before him, Hashem repaired everything in Kupayeh: harnesses, bicycles, cooking utensils, the pulleys used to draw water from the wells, samovars.

Hashem was in a state of confusion and distress following his wife's death. Firouzeh had been an impeccable housekeeper; everything in her house was clean and neat as a pin. But the young father, who had lost his mother when he was still very young, and never had a sister, was incapable of cooking and taking care of the children. The kadkhoda, Zahra, and the other villagers asked Soraya if she could help out, and she was happy to oblige.

Soraya had the time. It was therefore agreed among the villagers that she would go to Hashem's twice a day to help him with the housekeeping and cooking.

It was the opportunity to get rid of her that Ghorban-Ali had been waiting for. Each time he came back to the village he patiently followed Soraya, spying on her, tracking her to make sure she fell into the trap he was setting for her.

The young woman, completely unaware of what her husband was plotting, continued to visit Firouzeh's widower twice a day, to take care of his children, without, however, neglecting her own house and family.

By slow degrees, troublesome rumors began to circulate about Soraya from one end of the village to the other.

3

MAKING HIS WAY slowly toward the house of the kad-khoda, Sheik Hassan recalled the years just passed that had given his life a whole new turn. Everything had happened so quickly, so unexpectedly.

It was the shah's departure that had turned his world upside down. All of a sudden the people on the streets had seized power, and the prisons had emptied in the course of a single night. Mobs roamed the streets of the capital, thirsting for revenge and freedom. Madness and anarchy reigned, and the hooligans of the southern parts of the city had headed for the northern sectors, where the beautiful villas, major hotels, and chic restaurants were located.

In the Baghe Shah Military Prison, where he was incarcerated, Hassan Lajevardi had heard the shouts of the crowd and the noise of battle as the insurgents and the forces still faithful to the shah battled it out. Suddenly, the prison was surrounded, then stormed. From his cell window, Lajevardi could see the bodies of two soldiers that had been lying for hours in the snow of the prison courtyard, two dark spots on the white background.

There was the sound of keys rattling, the groaning of hinges as the cell doors swung open; the pounding of boots; then three persons armed with machine guns burst into the cell.

"How many of you in here?" a voice barked.

"Five," one of the prisoners responded.

"Line up facing me. And be quick about it!" the same person roared.

The man took three steps forward and surveyed the prisoners.

"Which of you knows how to read and write?"

Three of the five raised their hands.

"Which of you has a secondary school diploma? Anyone with a university education?"

Hassan Lajevardi responded affirmatively.

"What do you do with all that learning, you there, the old guy? You a professor?"

"No."

"You mean, 'No, sir!' " the man replied, raising his weapon a few inches higher toward the horizontal.

"No, sir. But I have my teaching diploma. I did a little teaching."

"Do you speak any foreign languages?"

"Turkish. And a little Arabic. And I have a smattering of English, though I don't claim to be fluent."

"How old are you?"

"Fifty-three, sir."

The man with the weapon took a step closer, till he was only inches from Hassan.

"So what brought you here? Are you a *savaki*?"

"No, sir. I'm here by mistake, I swear it."

The man burst out laughing. "You all say the same thing, you bunch of fascist cowards. Well, we'll see who's telling the truth. I'll take a look at your prison records in just a minute. And if you're lying, there'll be hell to pay!"

And with that he hit Hassan with the butt of his rifle in the small of the back, to move him down the hallway. Shortly thereafter, Hassan found himself in a huge, neon-lighted room filled with prisoners.

"All of you, sit down!" a voice bellowed. "And keep your mouths shut."

Throughout the morning, dozens of names were called, people were interrogated — even beaten if their answers proved less than satisfactory — then sent back to their cells. Now it was Hassan's turn. He felt worn out. He had had nothing to eat since the previous evening.

"Lajevardi! . . . Hassan Lajevardi!"

"That's me, sir," he responded, getting to his feet and approaching the raised platform where three armed men were seated, each dressed in battle fatigues and with a Palestinian kerchief around his neck.

"File number 7865/58. Swindling, fraud, forgery, utilization of forged papers, embezzlement, fraudulent bankruptcy, issuing checks without funds to cover same, resisting arrest, indecent exposure . . ."

The three judges looked at one another.

"Not bad for one person. You do all that by yourself?"

"I swear, gentlemen, I didn't do any of that. I told the other judge, but he didn't want to believe me."

"How long have you been in here?"

"Here at Baghe Shah? Ten days. But I was in the Ghasr Prison for seven months before that."

"You mean you were sentenced by one of the deposed shah's judges?"

"That is correct, sir."

"And why should we believe you?"

"Because it's all there, it's written in my record. I signed and dated the document."

The three judges murmured something under their breath to one another, then the one in the middle announced: "Would you like to work for us?"

"What does that mean exactly?" Hassan asked, taken aback by the offer.

"Do you want to work for the new republic that we're in the process of setting up, help us ferret out the royalists wherever they may be hiding?"

"Of course, of course I would. . . . In fact, I can tell you that in my own cell there are two of them . . . maybe even three!"

Thus it was that the new career began for Hassan Lajevardi, a career whose ascent was meteoric: scribe, interpreter, police informer, undercover agent for the new police, assistant to the hangman, spokesman for the public prosecutor of the revolution, and last but not least, representative of the ayatollah himself in a village in the northern part of the country. All that in the space of two years.

Hassan succeeded in making compromising files that implicated him vanish into thin air and in forging new files for himself that were pure as the driven snow. Sentenced a number of times for embezzlement and minor violations of the law, he eliminated all traces of his past, without, however, giving up his old identity.

He completely changed the way he looked: turban, long tunic, a light coat over his shoulders, *guivehs* on his feet, Koran and prayer beads in his hands, tinted glasses perched on the bridge of his nose — all gave him an intellectual and professorial look.

Up till this point in his life, Hassan had been a confirmed bachelor, but now he desired not only that he should marry but that, because of his new, exalted station, he should marry well. He chose a young, wealthy widow who owned a large house overlooking the sea, and vast plantations of rice and tea. He outfitted himself with a chauffeured car, upgraded his priestly vestments, purchased an illuminated Koran even embellished with a few precious stones. His comfortable new life might have gone on forever if an important Shiite dignitary had not stopped in one day to pay his respects to his colleague. The traveler was surprised and dismayed to note the comfort and opulence with which Hassan had surrounded himself, a situation hardly in keeping with the religious principles of the revolution. The only man in a spacious house, Lajevardi lived there with not only his wife and two step-daughters, but also his mother-in-law, two servants, and a neighbor who looked after the garden.

When the dignitary entered the house, Hassan was stretched out on a hammock. Two girls were fanning him with long palm branches. Before long the two men were arguing heatedly, and a month later the ayatollah's representative was stripped of his functions, and all his goods and possessions were summarily seized. Since he did not possess anything officially, it was easy for him to slip out of the village one morning, under the

36

pretense of visiting a neighboring town. In fact, he had stolen from his wife, while he was granting her her freedom. Gold rings, necklaces, bracelets, pendants, earrings, and hard cash had been quickly gathered together and tossed into a sack, and without any problem he had been able to hop on the bus that was just leaving for Chalous.

Lajevardi was a sexual pervert. After the shah's police learned that he took an uncommon, and doubtless unnatural, interest not only in the young girls but also in the young boys in his classes, he was dismissed from several different schools, then ultimately barred by the Ministry of Education from teaching altogether. He lived from hand to mouth, slept wherever he could, and it was thus that he was arrested and sentenced to prison several months before the revolution.

After having spent two years living on the Caspian shore, he fled now to the south, making sure to avoid the holy city of Qhom.

He lived the following two years at Yazd. A former Zoroastrian city that had converted to Islam, Yazd was situated on the edge of the desert. This commercial crossroads suited Hassan perfectly, for his major concern was to keep a low profile until the authorities had forgotten him.

For a while he was the handyman at the Mosque of Time and the Hour, then guide at the Chamseddine Mausoleum, before marrying again, this time the widow of a man who had been executed for collaborating with the old regime.

In this holy and lively city, he preferred to remain the civilian he should always have been, and let his new wife provide for his every need. This life might have gone on forever had it not been for the fact that one day Hassan was recognized by a former inmate of the Ghasr Prison, a man with whom he had actually shared a cell for several months.

In these small provincial towns, everyone knows everyone else's business, and before the sun had gone down the whole section of town in which Lajevardi lived had learned that the two men had known each other in prison, that they had been arrested for fraud, and that they had been set free only because of the revolution.

Divorced once again — and enriched once again by the minor theft committed in his ex-wife's closet — Hassan headed farther south, without a clear destination in mind, just so it put him as far from his past as possible.

Thus it was that one evening he arrived in Kerman, suitcase in hand filled with his clothes, a copy of the Koran, and a few jewels. Once again, he was a guide, this time in the Castle of the Green Dome and at the Pahenar Mosque, before landing a better-paying job as teacher at the Saadat School, in the eastern sector of the city. He taught the Holy Scriptures, as well as the life of the Prophet and his family. It was during this period that he saw the light and found his true vocation. Having a smattering of Arabic, he learned all the verses of the Koran by heart, voraciously read the Islamic newspapers and magazines, and learned the terms and phraseology of the pious people of whom he had hitherto been completely ignorant. Although he remained a layman, he felt himself irresistibly becoming a vicar of the Prophet.

At that time, Hassan was living in a rented room in a private house. He ate with the family who owned the house and even gave private lessons to the youngest son. His gray hair, his elegant beard, his imposing figure — for he was tall — made him look like the serious-minded person he aspired to be. But behind his tinted glasses, Hassan watched and waited, always on the lookout, like a bird of prey.

Far from the capital and its courts of revolutionary justice, Hassan lived from day to day, trying his best to make the people among whom he lived think well of him, and doing his best to ingratiate himself with the imam of the Friday Mosque, which he attended regularly.

The mosque had become the center for all matters of business, and all compromises, that took place in the city. Everything was settled in the vicinity of the central fountain in the courtyard, at certain hours between two prayers and three sermons: a petition to be brought before the authorities, the closing of a mortgage on a piece of property, a prompt divorce. Everything was for sale; everything could be bought; everything could be rented.

Over the fourth cup of tea, someone would deign to listen to you, while an envelope, stuffed with a few bank notes, was furtively passed from one hand to the other until it came to its final resting place somewhere in the ample folds of the ecclesiastical garb.

From as far back as he could remember, Hassan had been a master at the art of obsequiousness and the art of scheming. He had practiced both arts in times past with the directors of the schools where he had taught, with the people of authority in the former regime, and, more recently, with his prison guards. He was also unquestionably an expert in the fine art of flattery.

Little by little, he gained people's confidence and soon found himself taking the initiative or settling certain matters.

He knew how to make himself indispensable, and his greatest recompense for services rendered was to be invited to dine by the head of the mosque. People of modest means, hearing or knowing of his connections, pleaded with him to intercede on their behalf either with the political authorities or with the religious hierarchy, and thus he began to earn his first rials in the role of intermediary.

The sums quickly multiplied, although they were much smaller than those earned by truly influential people who frequented the mosque or the governor's palace. But Hassan knew how to bide his time. Extremely mistrustful, like so many people who slowly but surely climbed up the rungs of society one by one, Hassan had no confidence in banks, and preferred to keep his money on his person, trading it in for gold coins when the wads of paper money became too burdensome. He had a money belt made — it cost him a pretty penny — consisting of several compartments that locked by pressing on them, in which he stuffed his loot. He never separated himself from this new accoutrement, not even when he went to the public baths, not even when he slept.

When the president of Parliament, who had been born in Kerman, came to pay a visit to his fellow citizens, Hassan made a point of always being in a position of prominence. The gala celebration in the president's honor lasted for three days. On the eve of his departure, the dignitary asked to meet several local notables who had been of service to the revolution and to the aya- tollah. And so Hassan found himself in the wood-paneled main room of police headquarters, together with a few hundred other civil and religious leaders — the elite of the city — none of whom he knew.

When it came time for him to be introduced to the president, the prior of the Friday Mosque introduced Hassan with these words: "May I introduce Hassan Lajevardi, a man of piety, honesty and integrity, an excellent member of society and a remarkable peda- gogue."

The president smiled at him and said: "Congratula- tions on your good work. May it continue; you are a fine example for our youth. Our children need teachers such as yourself."

Hassan thanked him profusely, bowing respectfully and stammering: "Your Excellency. . . . I do my best. . . . May God and our beloved imam help me in my tasks."

By the time he straightened up, the president of Par- liament was already gone. Photographs had been taken, and the next day Hassan bought a dozen. You never knew: they might come in handy some day! Never had he felt so pleased with himself. . . .

From that moment on, no demonstration or official celebration took place without Hassan having been in- vited. The mayor befriended him and gave him a number of tasks to perform. But how can a crook — even one who has seen the light and repented — not be tempted

41

once someone has put into his hand an official letterhead, official stamps, an official automobile, and an intimate knowledge of the city's finances?

For a time, Hassan was able to keep temptation at bay, but the people who begged for his favors and were prepared to pay him for each service rendered ultimately won out over his recent and still very fragile integrity. From then on, he began to hand out illegitimate favors and privileges with disconcerting ease.

Until one day when he committed an error. He authorized the construction of a house on an empty lot that nobody seemed to claim and that he had appropriated to himself. In the course of the transaction, he had received a considerable sum of money. Everything would have gone off as planned if not for the mayor's secretary, who informed him a few days later that the so-called abandoned lot actually belonged to her family.

"You sold something that didn't belong to you," the secretary told him.

"This vacant lot was sold to me last month," Hassan responded, "and I resold it shortly thereafter to the party that owns it now."

"All your paperwork is phony. You clearly drew it up yourself."

The inquiry did not take long, and the resulting scandal was enormous. Hassan was immediately arrested and thrown into prison. He was left to stew there for two weeks, until the chief prosecutor for the Islamic republic in the region summoned him to his office.

"To steal from the State, to cheat God, to betray the revolution were your sole ambitions for the past several years. You tried to erase your abject past, but the members of my judicial staff were able to put all the missing pieces back together again. The nation is suffering, and paying with blood to defend its soil against the infidel encroachments from without, and all you were trying to do was to become wealthy at the expense of your brothers. You don't even deserve the bullet that will kill you."

Hassan Lajevardi lowered his head, unable to meet the prosecutor's gaze.

"You have nothing to say for yourself? Do you confess to your misconduct?"

"Yes, sir, I do. I have nothing to say."

There was a heavy silence. He saw the prosecutor nervously turning the pages of his file, read a few lines, lift his head, then bury himself again in the pile of papers.

"You still have nothing to say for yourself?"

"No, sir, I have nothing to say, except to implore your mercy and ask for leniency."

The man stared fixedly at him. His turban seemed to stay on his head only by virtue of two huge ears that stuck out on either side of his face. He could not have been more than thirty years old. His beard, such as it was, was thin and scraggly, and he resembled those harmless eunuchs one used to see in old miniature paintings.

"You mean to say you don't even have any proposal to make to me, no deal to suggest that might warrant my leniency?"

Hassan suspected that this was where the conversation was leading. He had been expecting such a question, and his answer had been prepared for two weeks. "I don't own much, but the little I do I am willing to put

43

at the disposal of the revolution and of your esteemed department."

"And precisely how much, may I ask, does that contribution amount to?"

"A few gold coins that I have been able to put aside from the money I've earned from my teaching since I first arrived in this city. It's not much, but I would proudly hand it over for the great national cause."

The prosecutor tapped his pencil against the file. His lips betrayed a wry smile. He remained silent for a good minute, all the while staring at the accused.

"Where is that money?"

"I have a little of it with me; the rest is in the bank."

"Show me what you have on you."

Slowly Hassan opened his belt and took out twelve *pahlavis*, which he placed on the judge's table. The man counted them.

"Are you sure that's all you have on you?"

"Yes, that's everything. . . . You can check if you like." And he handed him the belt.

"I believe you. . . . As for the rest, how long will it take you to get it to me?"

"As quickly as you like."

Hassan had amassed so many gold pieces over the past few months that he had had to empty his money belt, which had become too heavy to wear. He had buried his little hoard under a tree situated on a piece of land he had bought just at the edge of the city.

"This must all be done with the utmost discretion," said the prosecutor. "But I can't trust you. How do you suggest we go about it?"

The teacher suggested that the judge allow him to

44

go to the bank on his own so that he could withdraw his capital, and after that he would bring it to him at a designated place.

"Do you have a place in mind?" said the prosecutor.

Hassan told him about his little garden at the edge of town where no one ever came by, especially at nightfall. The man hesitated for a moment, then agreed.

"Don't try to pull a fast one on me," he said. "I intend to have you followed from the moment you leave here. Make sure you don't try to make the mistake of running away."

Hassan had spotted, almost since he had first arrived in Kerman, a branch office of the National Bank in the center of town that would suit his purposes perfectly. It was decided that he would withdraw his funds toward noon, and that the exchange would take place the same evening in Hassan's garden.

To go into the bank and emerge a half hour later carrying a package tied up with string was child's play for a seasoned crook like Hassan, who had noticed that he was indeed being followed. After leaving the bank, Hassan had no trouble losing himself in the crowd. Now all he had to do was quietly await the end of the day.

Toward nine o'clock that evening, an automobile drove up to Hassan's garden, then came in through the rusty gate, which was quickly closed behind it. It was a peaceful place, surrounded by high walls. In one corner, a little shed housed furniture and some garden tools.

The prosecutor had come alone. Hassan had expected he would. A sum of money such as this was not to be shared.

45

"It's a very pretty spot," the prosecutor said. "Very peaceful, as you said. How long ago did you buy it?"

"Not long ago. I come here sometimes with friends, when the heat of the city is too intense and when I feel a bit tired. I don't own a car myself, but walking has never been a problem for me."

The Islamic magistrate wanted to get the business over with. "I'm in a hurry. Can we settle the matter without further delay?"

"Of course, Your Honor. . . . It's over here; please be so kind as to follow me."

The magistrate fell in behind him. Everything happened very fast. No sooner had the man entered the shed when the teacher seized a pickax and hit the prosecutor on the head with all his might. There wasn't a scream, not even a moan; the only sound was that of the body falling to the ground. In the course of the afternoon, Hassan had dug a hole deep enough to contain the curled-up body of a man. With an expert hand, Hassan stripped the magistrate of his cleric's clothes, doing his best not to sully them further. He tossed the man's body into the pit and covered it with quicklime. Half an hour later, the hole was filled up and covered with the furniture and garden tools.

Hassan locked the door of the shed. He got into the prosecutor's car and drove about half a mile to the north, with the headlights out, in the direction of Ravar. When he reached the bridge, he got out of the car, put it in gear, and sent it tumbling into the raging waters of a stream a hundred feet below.

At the first light of dawn, he arose and wasted no

time washing away the last spots of blood from the prosecutor's turban and clothes. From the promontory where he had stationed himself, he dominated the countryside. No one could see him or take him by surprise. When the clothes were dry, he put them on, after having taken possession of the wallet, the watch, and other personal effects of his victim; then he dug a hole in which he buried his own clothes. He burned all the compromising papers belonging to the magistrate.

Only then did he ask himself what he planned to do next. Where in the world could he go now? Surely by now the alarm had been sounded. He had disappeared from the prison, so had the prosecutor. Before long they would have found the car. They would interrogate the peasants of Ravar, of Darband, or even of Nehbandan, at the gates of the desert.

He remembered that he had gone on a picnic one day with the family he had been living with in Kerman. The road they had taken ran along the other side of the mountain and ascended deep mountain gorges to the foot of soaring cliffs. But that day the weather had suddenly changed for the worse, and it had been impossible to reach the goal of their expedition, the village of Kupayeh. They had had to turn back and head home.

He was still a good twenty miles from Kupayeh. He decided that this was where he would go, and he began to walk.

As luck would have it, less than a half hour after he started off, an old bus drove past him and stopped. The driver leaned out of his window. "Come on, holy one, get in, I'll take you."

Hassan was caught off guard. If he refused, it would look suspicious. "I'm coming," he said. "How much will the fare be?"

The driver laughed. "On my bus God doesn't pay. He's our invited guest."

Hassan took a seat in the back of the bus. There were eight passengers on board, all burdened with various and sundry packages and small crates. They were all drowsing and paid no attention to him.

Half an hour later the bus pulled up and stopped in Kupayeh. It was market day.

Like a powder trail, news of the cleric's arrival in town spread through the village. To be sure, from time to time a cleric showed up in Kupayeh, but only on special occasions. Where did this one come from? And where was the kadkhoda? Why wasn't he there to greet the holy man?

The son of the well digger ran as fast as his legs could carry him in search of the kadkhoda.

"Machdi Ebrahim! Machdi Ebrahim!"

He rushed into the town hall where he saw Shokrollah Jalili, one of Ebrahim's deputies.

"Is the kadkhoda here?

"He's down in the meadow."

The child found the kadkhoda seated in the grass next to the shepherd, puffing on his pipe that was his constant companion.

"Machdi Ebrahim . . . come . . . come right away."

The old man lifted his head: "What's the matter, Rahim. Why are you in such a hurry?"

"Come," the boy repeated. "Right now." And he took

the kadkhoda's hand and tried to help him to his feet. "He's here! He's here!"

"But what's this all about? Tell me what you're trying to say, child."

"The mullah . . . the mullah! . . . He came on the bus with Nasrollah."

Ebrahim had great difficulty keeping up with the boy's pace. When they reached the town square, the market was in full swing, but there was no sign of any mullah.

"Tell me, Nasrollah, what's this all about? Did you bring a mullah with you?"

"Yes, Kadkhoda, there was a mullah, who wasn't very talkative with me. I didn't charge him any fare. God will reimburse me someday. He went in that direction. He wanted to know who was in charge in the village."

The mayor and the child backtracked and headed toward the town hall. As soon as they entered they saw Hassan Lajevardi. His back was turned to them. He was seated at a table, waiting for Shokrollah to serve him.

"*Salam al leikum,*" said Ebrahim.

The cleric returned his greeting, adding: "May Almighty God protect you, you and all your people."

The mayor inclined slightly forward, as a sign of respect and to thank him, then said: "You are welcome among us, Holy One. . . . The little we have is yours."

Shokrollah poured him some tea and offered him a few dried cakes and some fruit. The stranger drank noisily and downed the proffered food voraciously. He had eaten nothing since the previous evening, and the momentous events of the past twenty-four hours had made him inordinately hungry. When he had eaten and

49

drunk to his fill, he straightened up, wiped his mouth with the back of his hand, and said: "My name is Hassan Lajevardi, and I travel throughout the country from one end to the other, in the name of the imam, to spread his word and the word of God."

They all took stock of this man of haughty bearing, with his glasses perched at the end of his long nose, with his bountiful grizzled beard and, on his head, the well-known black turban of the *seyeds*, who were related to the family of the Prophet. His long, light-brown robe, which looked almost new, fell to his bare feet, which were laced in sandals. Ebrahim, Shokrollah, and little Rahim all intoned as one: "Glory to God and to his Prophet. . . . Long life to our revered imam."

"I have just come from Kerman, and before that I was at Yazd, and before Yzad at Ispahan, and even before that I was at Qhom, our holy city."

"Let this place be yours, Your Eminence," said the mayor. "We are people of modest means, but we are honest and hardworking. Ask, and you shall receive whatever you desire. It is God Who has sent you to be among us. You are most welcome."

"I am a widower. I am alone. All I want is a little human warmth among good and simple people."

Now everyone was eating and drinking. When the teapot was empty, Lajevardi broke the silence: "Down in the valley, people spoke very highly of you. So I made up my mind to pay you a visit and to remain here for a short while, before resuming my journey. Unfortunately, my stay here among you will be brief."

Machdi Ebrahim considered himself honored by such a visit. He gave him the best room in the town hall and that same evening introduced Hassan Lajevardi to the people of the village. Hassan quickly became an integral part of the village, thanks in large part to his obvious piety and devotion which were admired by one and all.

It did not take long for the kadkhoda to fall under the spell of his new guest. He sought out his company whenever possible; he loved to listen to the man tell of his many voyages, of his pilgrimage to Mecca, and of his personal meetings with the great imam in the country's capital.

When Ghorban-Ali arrived one evening in the village, and found himself face-to-face with the newcomer, there was a moment of silence; then following the usual pleasantries and introductions, the two men exchanged a few banalities. Only a practiced eye could have discerned that the two men knew each other.

A short while later, at the insistence of Ghorban-Ali, Ebrahim agreed to place the arbab's house at the cleric's disposal. Two village women were assigned to his service, and he who henceforth called himself Sheik Hassan became without question the most important person in Kupayeh.

As the months went by, the false cleric gained an increasing and visible ascendancy over the mayor and began to see to it that his wishes were not only known but carried out.

He knew how to flatter with great subtlety, how to direct even as he himself remained in the background, so that Machdi Ebrahim alone reaped the benefit of his, Hassan's, intrigues.

Nevertheless, the sheik quickly amassed a nice little stash, since his functions allowed him to act as notary

51

whenever the occasion demanded, as well as lawyer, go-between, usurer, and, quite naturally, as scribe and secret adviser to the entire community.

Thus the arbab's former house became a kind of law court where the mullah played all the roles, those of both prosecutor and public defender. And since any service rendered had its price, it was not long before the sheik had managed to acquire a few acres of land, half a dozen head of cattle, some poultry, one or two houses half in ruin, and, most important, possession of a field that ran along the stream from which both Kupayeh and the valley below derived their water supply.

All this was done by perfectly legal means, with the full accord of the mayor and his deputies. Zahra Khanum did her best to warn Ebrahim that this frightful character was not only a charlatan but a crook, but he would not hear a word of it, merely declaring that she knew nothing of the world of business, and that she should not worry her head about such things.

"Poor Ebrahim," Zahra would say to herself, "if only he had all his wits about him."

Ebrahim had left the village only once in his long life. Too poor to make the pilgrimage either to Mecca or Karbala, he had saved up, rial by rial, until he had put aside enough to pay for a trip to Machad, in celebration of his thirtieth birthday. That voyage to the other end of the country had lasted a month, and he returned home completely transformed by it. It was as though he had been touched by grace. He who till then had been restless and boisterous had become calm and thoughtful.

He, the vagabond, who had seemed to be interested in nothing, had made up his mind to study one hour a day at the local school, so that he could learn at least the rudiments of reading and numbers.

Upon his return from his pilgrimage, he was entitled to use the title *Machdi,* which gave him a certain prestige among the local administrators.

As chief magistrate of a village of two hundred and fifty souls, he was endowed with great power. From birth to death, he helped the villagers, all of whom were his friends. Not once did he ask for remuneration for his work, but he was not above accepting a chicken or a pound or two of rice for some task or favor he had done. So Zahra could not understand why Machdi Ebrahim had taken such a sudden and obvious interest in money since Hassan's arrival in the village.

There were times when Ebrahim and the mullah closeted themselves for hours on end in the former house of the landowner. No one could figure out what they could be discussing. Later on, Ghorban-Ali, whose various and sundry businesses down in Kerman were bearing fruit, and Hashem, the widower of Firouzeh, would come and join them.

Zahra, whose house was next to the arbab's, heard the sound of their voices, but she could not make out what they were plotting. She did, however, know without a doubt that under cover of Hassan's supreme authority, and with the unwitting complicity of the mayor, the four men were cooking up some scheme of a dubious nature. The voices she could hear most clearly were those of the mullah and Soraya's husband.

Zahra was astonished by one thing: the role of Machdi

53

Ebrahim. The man had never had any great desires. He owned his house; his children were all grown up and independent; his modest income sufficed for his needs; and since the death of his wife he had never even considered remarrying. Always humbly clothed, he had no real needs.

For a while now rumor had it that Ghorban-Ali wanted to remarry a young woman from the city whom no one had ever seen. Soraya had not had relations with her husband for years now, and a divorce would not have affected her. The only thing was, if Ghorban-Ali did repudiate his wife, he would have to pay dearly for the separation, since Soraya was above reproach.

It was out of concern for her niece that the old woman waived her principles and one day made a point of calling out to the mayor on the village square, in a voice loud enough for everyone to hear: "Hey there, Ebrahim, when you've finished work, come on over and see me. And make it soon. I'll be waiting for you."

Never before had anyone ever heard Zahra Khanum invite someone from the village to come and see her at home, and certainly not with such a show of authority. The mayor stopped what he was doing, stared at his friend Zahra, then walked away.

Zahra yelled after him: "Don't forget . . . I'll be waiting for you."

Late that afternoon, Ebrahim knocked on Zahra's door.

"Come in," she called, "the door's open. . . . You took long enough to get here."

The mayor mumbled a few incomprehensible words, then sat down.

"Did you have to ask Mr. Lajevardi's permission before you came?" she asked. "In other words, you're no longer in charge in your own village?"

"Are you spying on me?"

"Why should I want to spy on you? All I have to do is look out my window, and there you are, at any time of the day or night, entering or leaving his house. In the old days, you used to spend more time at your own house, or at the town hall, or in the fields. Now it looks as if you live in that person's house."

"Still the same old venomous tongue, eh, Zahra? Won't you ever change?"

"Do you honestly think that two old crabs like you and me can change at our age? It's too late for that, and that's precisely what is bothering me, Machdi."

"What is bothering you?"

"That I no longer see in you, Ebrahim, what everyone used to love and respect. Since this character arrived in town, you are completely under his influence. I'm not talking about Ghorban-Ali or Hashem, who are more to be pitied than they are to be blamed. But you — at your age — I can't even conceive of what's got into you."

"But I'm still the same as I always was, Zahra. You know that's true."

"My poor friend, you think you're the same, but you're completely different. I don't know what you're doing with that man. I have a fairly good idea what it is, but let me tell you one thing, Machdi Ebrahim, kadkhoda though you may be, I will not allow you to harm or in any way hurt my little Soraya, because she is what this is all about, isn't it? The whole village knows it."

"The whole village knows what?"

55

"Knows that you're cooking up some plot having to do with Ghorban-Ali and Soraya."

Ebrahim replied to her calmly: "It's true that Ghorban-Ali wants to marry a lovely girl who lives down in the city, and move to Kerman. It's also true that his wife no longer gives him satisfaction. And I will go even farther and say that he has a long list of justified complaints against Soraya. She is less and less attentive to him; she no longer takes good care of their children, the food she serves him is becoming almost inedible; and he finds that she's spending a bit too much time at Hashem's since Firouzeh died."

Zahra cut him off short: "Ebrahim Lahouti, look me squarely in the eye. . . . Do you realize what you have just said? Aren't you ashamed of yourself? There is not a better wife and mother in this entire village than Soraya, and you know it!"

"We are all of the opinion that she goes to Hashem's too often, and that she stays there too long each time she goes."

"But we all asked her to do that," Zahra protested. "No one wanted to take on the task. We all chose Soraya. You mean you don't remember? Ebrahim, look me in the eye: do you or do you not remember? In fact, it was you who accompanied her to his house the first time she went there!"

The old man lowered his head and said nothing.

"I want to know what's going on!"

"This is men's business, not women's. And besides, you wouldn't understand if I told you."

"And you mean to tell me you understand? With characters like Hassan and Ghorban-Ali, that's some team you all make: you; a widower; a so-called mullah; and a ne'er-do-well."

"I forbid you to talk like that. Mr. Lajevardi is a man of God, and you must respect him as such. The man is blameless, and you have no right to say such things about him. He does honor to our village."

"You know you're lying, Ebrahim. But he has you so wrapped around his little finger that you're no longer the same person. I'm not ashamed of you; I'm ashamed for you."

The old woman was all wound up, and nothing could stop her.

"In the space of a few months you've lost everything, everything that gave you the right to be the head of our community: authority, honesty, courage, independence, goodness. . . . Just look at you, if you still have enough guts to look at yourself in the mirror. For a long time you've no longer been the real kadkhoda of the village, and I'm not the only one who thinks so. The whole village agrees with me. And we're all overwhelmed by it. I'm warning you, Machdi Ebrahim, for I'm the only person here who still dares talk to you this way: don't push this too far; otherwise you'll find me blocking your path, the way you've found me standing in your path many times in the past. . . . Do you remember? . . . Do you?"

Soraya had paid little or no attention to the plot which was being hatched in the former house of the arbab. She knew she was blameless, as both Ghorban-Ali and Hashem could attest. Yet Zahra tried to forewarn her.

"You must be careful," she said. "Both Ghorban-Ali and Hashem are not the same people they used to be. Ever since Hashem has been alone, he follows your husband like a faithful dog. He's completely under his influence. He'll side with whoever and whatever strikes him as in his best interest. Firouzeh is no longer here to guide him. And since your husband has taken to spending time down in Kerman, he's passed on to us all the city's bad habits."

Soraya did not respond. She knew that the old woman was right, but even so, what could she do about it? She no longer talked with her husband and hadn't for some time now. Her two oldest boys avoided her. As for the younger children, they were growing up in the street, only returning home, dusty and dirty, when the sun had gone down behind the mountains.

Weighed down by the hostility she felt building up all around her, the young woman one day decided simply to stop speaking. Seeing the course Soraya had adopted, Zahra realized that it would be even more difficult now to take her defense, as long as Soraya refused to explain her position.

As for Hassan Lajevardi, he lacked nothing, least of all food. Those who took care of him were in the habit of bringing him each and every morning a liter of milk, some cheese, and bread. Coddled, he was also handsomely rewarded for all the services he rendered.

Thus, from his myriad underhand transactions, he had acquired an impressive little nest egg for himself, which soon made him one of the most important landowners

58

in the entire mountain region. This process was accelerated because for his various operations he had dealings, through the intermediary Ghorban-Ali, with the hooligans down in the valley. But as always he managed to keep a very low profile, and his name never appeared anywhere; it sufficed that he was in control. It was Soraya's husband who signed and initialed all the official documents, and the deed, whatever it was, was done.

So it was that Ghorban-Ali became the happy owner of a little garden on the outskirts of the city, a tree-filled garden with a little tool shed in one corner. As a result of all this wheeling and dealing, Machdi Ebrahim also became the owner of several shares of a whorehouse he had one day visited, without, however, having succumbed to the temptations of the flesh.

Everyone made deals of one kind or another while, behind the scenes, Hassan pulled all the strings.

The person manipulated the most was without doubt Machdi Ebrahim. As mayor of the village, he enjoyed an indisputable authority in the community, and the official seals he affixed to any and all documents legalized, as it were, the illicit commerce that Sheik Hassan was carrying on in league with Ghorban-Ali.

The mullah drew up documents and official texts as he saw fit. No one could contest what he did, first of all because not many people in the village knew how to read or write but also because those few who did were soon thrown off by the vocabulary of officialdom.

The kadkhoda let himself be taken in. He signed every paper put in front of him, playing his role as village leader to the hilt, and he accepted the insults that Zahra continued to shower upon him as so many encouragements to stay on the path that Hassan had laid out for him.

No one seemed to take any interest in these business transactions, and when upon occasion Ghorban-Ali's two oldest sons, Hussein-Ali and Hassan-Ali, referred to what was going on, or asked questions, the quartet had ready answers for everything. Even Hashem turned out to be a perfect accomplice. All they asked of him was that he accuse Soraya, that he confirm that she was badgering him, pestering him, in fact making indecent proposals to him. He was also to say that on several occasions she had openly tried to seduce him, that she had even caressed and fondled him and had used words that a married woman says to her husband and to him alone.

What the mayor wanted to avoid at all costs was to appear dishonest in the eyes of Zahra, who, he knew, was following his every move from behind her windows. He knew that she knew, and he therefore did his best to keep up appearances and, insofar as it was possible, to save face with her.

For more than fifty years this woman had dominated him; she had always demanded, and always obtained, whatever she wanted from him. He had never known how to say no to her, but today he would know how to face up to her simply because he had no other choice. The plot had been set in motion. It fit in with his own interests as well as those of Hassan. Above all, he did not want to have the slightest problem with that man, who in the bare blink of an eye had taken over the whole village. Had he been sent here by someone? Did he really have, as he claimed, close connections in high places? Could he, as he was wont to repeat, call on the local police, or the national security forces, or even an Islamic judge whenever it so pleased him?

Throughout his life Ebrahim had been weak. He had responded to the demands of the arbab by bowing and remaining silent. Confronted with the eccentricities of his wife, who came to Kupayeh without wearing the veil, he had said nothing. And faced with his son's provocations, his son who was flirting outrageously with the girls of the village in defiance of tradition, he again chose silence as his recourse.

But since Zahra was making a point of provoking and humiliating him at the slightest opportunity, well, this time she would see what he was made of.

Nothing could stand in his way, and as soon as Hassan and Ghorban-Ali, aided and abetted by Hashem, could prove Soraya's guilt and make it all public, he, Machdi Ebrahim, would confirm what they said and take the matter to its conclusion.

4

ZAHRA, THE FEMALE ELDER of the village, was a wizened old woman bowed down with the ordeals of age. No one knew exactly how old she was — just as no one was quite certain how old Machdi Ebrahim was — but they were both well beyond three score and ten. Everyone feared Zahra, but all were nonetheless anxious for her respect.

For decades now, no decision was made without her approval. Whether it was a question of clearing the forests or building a bridge over the neighboring stream or digging deeper wells; whether it was a matter of marriages or funerals, she always had a strong opinion on the subject.

Wise men came to her to solicit her opinion, and everyone knew that Machdi Ebrahim, whose father had been the mayor of the village before him, did not have the qualities it took to succeed his father when the old man died. Yet Zahra decided that he should be mayor, and no one dared to dispute her.

Ever since she was a little girl, Zahra had gone, in good weather and bad, to do the family washing at the stream.

She divided her time between the stream and her house, saying little, listening carefully, and seeing everything. Aside from her family, few visitors crossed her threshold.

Zahra knew every last detail of the private lives of all of Kupayeh's inhabitants; she officiated at the births and circumcisions, took aside the naive young men of the village, the night before their marriages, and informed them how to conduct themselves. One after the other, she had buried all her childhood friends. She had never had any desire to go down to the big city, but she knew all about what went on in Kerman from the stories people brought back to her.

The days the bus arrived in the village sent her into hiding, and she was barely interested in the Thursday afternoon visits of the arbab and his family. The days of *sizda bedar* — the thirteenth day after *nowruz* — when all the villagers left the town as tradition required, she remained alone in her house. Then the village was all hers, and she wandered to and fro among the empty houses, with only a few stray dogs, the crows in the trees, and the first butterflies that appeared each spring as her companions.

For several years now she had no longer taken part in the collective festivities, not even the marriages. Only when there were funerals could she be seen heading toward the tiny cemetery situated in the nearby forest, to bid some friend a final farewell. Her father had sunk the village's first well, and she had been given the honor of drawing the first water. Since then, the spot bore her name.

All Zahra knew was the village and the surrounding area. She had always lived in the same house, right next to the arbab's, which she had inherited from her father. From the time she was a little girl, she had always been self-reliant and shown a rare independence of mind.

In those days, girls did not go to school. They stayed home and helped their mother with the household chores; then, when they were still very young, they were married off to some neighbor, an arrangement that sometimes allowed two parcels of land to be stitched back together, or for a hovel to be improved and enlarged.

During Zahra's childhood, an itinerant teacher arrived from the city in a cart drawn by a mule. He brought with him colored pencils, some books, and a flute. He spent several days in the village, and of all the pupils in his improvised course, Zahra was the most diligent.

Her interest in knowledge never left her, only increasing with the years, and later she taught what she had retained, for, she said: "God and his Prophet knew how to read and write, and any decent Muslim ought to be able to as well."

One day Zahra's parents decided she was old enough to get married; they chose Morteza for her, but she wouldn't have him. She ran away, spending hours on end wandering in the fields, and when she returned to the house at dusk she explained that she did not want to marry any boy who could neither read nor write.

She ultimately settled for Nematollah, who was ten years her senior and had shown a certain disposition for reading and numbers. In fact, with the help of Zahra, he became the kadkhoda's right arm, looking after all the paperwork and archives of the village.

As a young bride, Zahra had the same lot as all the other village girls. Over the next ten years she was pregnant several times, giving birth to six children. Only one of these children, who balked at the idea of remaining a peasant for the rest of his life, went off to the city. He became a policeman.

She remained Nematollah's spouse for over thirty years. She became a widow only a short time before the death of Machdi Ebrahim's wife. Everyone in the village assumed that these two old friends would end up getting married. But nothing ever came of it, and life went on as before.

Aside from her house and family, and her regular trips to the stream, Zahra seemed uninterested in anything. One by one she married off her children, but none of them remained nearby. Opinionated as she was, sticking her nose into everybody's business, Zahra made life impossible, though in her view just the opposite was true.

Very early on in her life, Zahra had shown a marked preference for her niece Soraya. She alone was allowed to visit her aunt at any time of the day, without having to let her know in advance that she was coming. Ghorban-Ali dreaded his wife's visits to the old lady, for he was sure that she complained about him to Zahra, about his laziness, his lack of cleanliness, his lies. Zahra was renowned for her outbursts of anger, and Ghorban-Ali sorely dreaded them.

Like Zahra, Soraya had a basic education, and she tried to pass it on to her children. Like Zahra, she was an impeccable housekeeper, and brought her children up to be neat and clean. Like Zahra, she did not linger in the village streets and spoke to no one unless spoken to.

And when it became clear that Ghorban-Ali preferred life down in the plain, Soraya found at the old lady's the comfort and counsel she sought.

This particular morning Zahra was in her kitchen when she suddenly heard a great commotion outside, some-one screaming and shouting. It was market day, and the cries of the vendors reached her ears. But these were louder shouts and caught her attention. She went over to the window and leaned out. A crowd had gathered only a few steps from her house. The old woman was straining to try to figure out who was the object of all the shouting.

"Whore . . . that's all you are, a filthy whore! A bitch . . . daughter of a bitch!"

Zahra was finally able to recognize the voice of Ghor-ban-Ali. Somewhat taken aback, she hesitated for a moment, then made up her mind to go out and approach the crowd.

The shouts were growing louder: "Prostitute . . . daughter of a prostitute! . . . Shame on you, you shame-less woman!"

With great difficulty, she shouldered her way through the crowd and saw Soraya surrounded by a group of men and woman, all of whom were screaming and brow-beating her. The young woman tried to escape the en-raged assembly, but they began lashing out at her and she fell under a rain of blows.

Zahra hurled herself into the mob and tried to protect her niece. She, too, was struck as several people lashed out at her as well.

"Keep out of this Zahra Khanum; this whore doesn't deserve your protection. . . . Let us handle the matter by ourselves."

The two women got to their feet, and everyone fell silent. Then Zahra, taking stock of Ghorban-Ali, said to him: "What exactly is going on here? Have you gone crazy? Do you have any idea what you're doing?"

"She's only getting what she deserves. . . . She's been unfaithful to me. . . . Do you realize that? Unfaithful!" In a state of rage, he was having great difficulty controlling himself.

"What do you mean she's been unfaithful to you? When was she unfaithful? Where? And with whom?"

"Right now. Over there, with Hashem. I caught them in the act."

"He's right," screamed the crowd. "Ghorban-Ali's telling the truth. She's been unfaithful to him."

Zahra still didn't understand.

"Stop shouting this way. I can't make out a word you're saying when everyone's shouting at once. Come over to my house, and let's get to the bottom of this."

She took Soraya by the shoulder, followed by her husband and about twenty villagers.

When they reached her house she turned to the crowd. "You're not all coming in," she said. "Only Soraya and Ghorban-Ali. Someone go and fetch the kadkhoda. I don't want anyone else here!"

The crowd remained in front of the house, awaiting

the arrival of Machdi Ebrahim. Soraya was in tears, and Ghorban-Ali, standing next to her, was trembling with rage.

When the mayor arrived, he started to question the old lady. "So what's this all about? What's going on?"

Before Zahra had a chance to reply, Ghorban-Ali shouted: "She's betrayed me. She betrayed me with Hashem. I knew it all along. And now I just caught them in the act."

Ebrahim turned to Soraya and asked: "Is it true what your husband says? Did you betray him?"

She made an effort to speak. "No," she said, "it's not true. I didn't betray him."

Once again her husband began to shout at the top of his lungs: "You're lying . . . you're lying. Admit that you're lying; the whole village knows you're lying. You go to Hashem's house every day; you take better care of him and his house than you do of your own family. You've slept with him. Everybody knows that."

"That's not true. . . . Why are you saying that? Zahra Khanum, you know the truth. Don't let him say such things!"

Soraya was clinging to the old lady's arm, an imploring look on her face.

Zahra, very moved by what she had just heard from her niece, began to question Soraya's husband: "You say that she's betrayed you. Just what has she done?"

"She knows what she's done. I saw them standing close to each other. I saw them whispering together. I caught them.. . . . She's guilty . . . she's betrayed me."

Ebrahim broke in: "Soraya, is your husband telling the truth?"

The young woman was so upset, and her sobs so strong, that she had trouble trying to give her side of the story. "I told Hashem that I had prepared his supper, that I had done the laundry, and that tonight I would take the children's clothes home to iron. We did smile at each other. You all know that since Firouzeh died I've been taking care of her family. Everyone knows that."

"The same way everyone knows that you stay at his house for hours on end, that you sleep with him. People even say you're pregnant by him."

"That's a lie! I've never touched Hashem, and he's never touched me. How, as a married woman, would I dare do such a thing?"

Somewhat skeptical, Ebrahim said: "Soraya, we have known you ever since you were born. But it is also a fact that ever since our beloved Firouzeh went to her reward you have been spending a great deal of time at Hashem's house, and I can understand why your husband is complaining. You're neglecting your own house and your own children."

"I haven't neglected anyone. Ask Zahra Khanum, ask my neighbors. They'll tell you: I'm a good mother and a faithful wife."

"That's a lie! You betrayed me; the whole village knows it. You betrayed me when I was away at Kerman. Sheik Hassan knows it; he told me so. . . . Go ahead and ask him, Machdi Ebrahim."

Zahra replied: "To speak to the husband of your best girl friend is not an offense. Hashem is a good and decent man. Have him come here; he'll tell us the truth."

The widower was ushered into Zahra's house, and the

mayor began to question him: "Tell me, Hashem, what were you and Soraya saying to each other a little while ago, when you were whispering together?"

"She told me that she was going to come over to my house to prepare lunch, that she was going to iron my clothes . . . and . . . er . . ."

"What else, Hashem? Go on."

"And she said she'd like to take a little rest while she was there, that the market had tired her out."

"That's not what I said," cried Soraya. "I never said anything of the sort. What I said was that I was going to bring your laundry back to my house and that I would iron it as soon as I'd taken a nap."

Hashem bowed his head, refusing to respond further.

Ghorban-Ali picked up the thread. "You see, all she does is lie. She's always lied."

The kadkhoda, somewhat embarrassed, glanced over at Zahra, coughed awkwardly, and resumed: "Hashem, listen to me carefully; this is very important. Did Soraya say that she wanted to take a little rest at your house after lunch or did she not? Speak up!"

The man hesitated for a moment and, without lifting his head, glanced furtively at Ghorban-Ali, who was standing opposite him, directly behind the mayor.

"Hashem, answer my question. Yes or no?"

"Yes . . . yes, she did say it."

"Look me in the eye, and repeat what you have just said."

Hashem was a rough, somewhat loutish man. He could never bring himself to look people in the eye when he talked with them, and as soon as he was intimidated he inevitably lowered his head. The smallest annoyance or vexation could render him speechless for hours on end. Ebrahim knew that, but he wanted to get a clear-cut answer from him.

"Hashem, look at me closely. You're not afraid of me. We've known each other a long time. I'm like your father. I want you to look at me and answer yes or no."

The widower raised his head, carefully avoiding the gaze of the two women who were staring at him fixedly.

"I'm going to ask you one more time. Think carefully before you answer. Yes or no, did Soraya suggest that she would like to come and take a rest at your house after lunch? Yes or no?"

Ghorban-Ali made an imperceptible movement of his head, a nod, in the direction of his friend, a signal that Zahra noticed immediately. She sent a withering glance toward Soraya's husband, who in turn lowered his head.

"Yes, Machdi Ebrahim, she did say it.. . . . She wanted to do it the way she has often done it before. . . . She's forever coming over to my house. . . . I don't like it. . . . She lies down on the bed when nobody's there. . . . She says things to me that are embarrassing. . . . It's true, I'm telling the truth. . . . You must believe me!"

Soraya couldn't believe her ears.

"That's a lie! I've never stayed for a minute at Hashem's after my work is done. The door is always open. My God, what do I have to do for people to believe me? I swear before the Almighty; every word that Hashem has just said is a total lie!"

Then, turning toward the widower, she said to him:

71

"Why are you saying such things? You know that I love you like a brother and that Firouzeh was my sister. Why are you trying to hurt me this way?"

A heavy silence ensued, which lasted for several seconds. Then, after a discreet signal from Ghorban-Ali, Hashem reiterated his charge: "Machdi Ebrahim, everything I said is the truth; I swear it is. Soraya comes to my house all the time, even when I don't need her. Ghorban-Ali knows it; I told him about it. So does Sheik Hassan; I told him, too. And what I told both of them is the truth."

And then he bowed his head again, as if he were ashamed of what he had just said.

Ebrahim ran his fingers through his beard and, ignoring the presence of Zahra and Soraya, turned toward Ghorban-Ali and asked: "Is that true? You knew all about it?"

"Yes, Machdi Ebrahim, but I didn't want to believe it. I love my wife, and I couldn't believe what I heard. Sheik Hassan talked to me about it; others did, too, when I returned from Kerman, but I still didn't believe them. I had to see it with my own eyes; I had to actually see it happening. And today I did!"

"What did you see? Tell me once again."

"I saw them smiling together; I saw them whispering together; I saw them holding hands. She leaned over and whispered something in his ear. That's what I saw!"

Soraya chimed in once again: "I didn't lean over, and I didn't whisper. I didn't touch his hand. Maybe we did smile at each other; I don't remember. I smile at everyone at Kupayeh, men and women alike, if they're decent folk."

"Soraya, two men present in this room are accusing you of conduct unworthy of a wife and mother. Can you prove they're not telling the truth?"

The young woman, completely taken aback by the question, stammered: "Prove . . . what do you mean, prove? I have nothing to prove. They're the ones who have to furnish proof. Where? When? Under what circumstances? What answers do they have to those questions? I'm an honest woman; I have known only one man in my life, my husband. . . . I have nothing to prove, and if you are saying with the same malice that I'm pregnant, then all you have to do is wait for nine months and you'll see it's all a pack of lies!"

That last declaration seemed to irritate the mayor, who clearly was not expecting it. He resumed speaking: "Soraya, you seem to be unaware of the laws of our society such as they were promulgated by our revered imam several years ago. When a man accuses his wife, she has to prove her innocence. That is the law. On the other hand, if a woman makes an accusation against her husband, she has to produce proof. Do you understand? They say you are guilty. Prove the opposite, and we'll all believe you without any problem."

At that point, Zahra, who had been unusually silent, spoke up and said: "Ebrahim, we know each other too well to lie to each other, don't you agree? All right, what I'm saying to you is that this whole business smells of a plot. Soraya has nothing to prove. She is honest, hardworking, a good mother, and a fine, upstanding wife. Ever since Firouzeh died she has been helping out her friend's family. And you would like her to prove that she is faithful and hasn't betrayed her husband. But do you realize the absurdity of the situation? If it were one of your own daughters, would you be asking the same questions? Of course you wouldn't. You know very well that Soraya has done nothing, and you don't dare say it. Admit that what I am saying is true!"

Taken aback by the old woman's aggressive stance, the mayor let the storm blow over, then responded: "If one of my own daughters had allowed herself to be put in this same position — may God never allow it to happen — I would have acted in exactly the same way, you may be sure. As mayor of this village, I am bound to conduct this inquiry, whether you like it or not. This woman is accused of being unfaithful both by her husband and by this man people say is her lover. Sheik Hassan, our mullah, is apparently aware of the situation. Now I, too, am aware of it, and other people in the village as well. We shall be the judges."

And without even saying good-bye to the old woman, he turned and left her house, followed by Ghorban-Ali and Hashem. Outside, the villagers who had been waiting in front of Zahra's house scattered.

Zahra was so dumbfounded she could find no words to express what she was feeling. Soraya, dismayed and exhausted, had slumped to the floor. She was pale as a ghost, unable to move or utter a single word.

Suddenly Zahra was overcome with panic. She knew Soraya as well as she knew herself, and she was painfully aware that the woman was completely incapable of defending herself. She had always known it. Whenever, as a child, someone accused her of doing something stupid or silly, she always lowered her head and allowed herself to be punished without saying a word.

Zahra had never accepted the fact of male domination in the village. She never hesitated to speak her mind, and the men of the village were in awe of her and dreaded her tongue lashings.

But since the revolution, men had become all-powerful, and Zahra had had to admit defeat and let the new order have its way. Any effort on her part to obstruct, to take a definite stand or offer a strong opinion on a given subject, would have been misunderstood and automatically used against her, with all the consequences.

The day she saw Sheik Hassan arrive at Kupayeh, Zahra immediately knew that the Devil had entered the village and that no one would dislodge him from it. In the space of a very short time, the mullah, who had a certain amount of education and culture, had intrigued and made friends with all the men. In the evening, after their work, he talked to the villagers, enlightening them on their rights, their prerogatives, their privileges, and the limits beyond which women were no longer allowed to go. A number of hitherto anonymous and colorless villagers were metamorphosed virtually overnight and began to spread terror throughout the area with their knives and their slingshots.

Young women like Soraya or Firouzeh or Kokab became frightened and sought refuge in their houses until such time as Machdi Ebrahim had regained control of the situation. But the threat, far from disappearing, continued to grow, aided and abetted by a number of men in the village, most of whom were known to be both lazy and filled with anger, men who had found in a new Islam the purifying element that gave a sense to their wretched lives.

Sheik Hassan plowed through the only street in the village like a messiah come to bring the true and only Word to the people, but he quickly understood that in Zahra he would have a formidable opponent. The old woman never once invited him into her house, and their rare conversations were limited to such amenities as "with the help of God," "God willing," or "thanks be to God."

It did not take the septuagenarian long to become aware of the danger. She knew that Hassan had made advances to Soraya which had been rejected; she also knew that Ghorban-Ali was having an affair in the city and that he would stoop to anything to repudiate his wife without having to return her dowry.

"Soraya, now that we're alone, tell me the truth. Has there been anything at all going on between you and Hashem?"

The young woman raised her head and looked at her aunt with the same ingenuous expression she had always had whenever she didn't understand, or whenever she feared, something.

"Aunt Zahra," she said, "how can you even ask me such a question?"

"I am asking it because I want an answer."

"Never, Aunt Zahra. I never did anything with

Hashem or with any other man. You know it, and every-one else does, too. Even the thought of doing such a thing has never entered my head, because I was raised by my mother and father never to have such thoughts. I am an honorable woman, and I shall be one to the end of my days."

"I wanted to hear you say it, that's all."

She laid her hand on Soraya's head and blessed her. "May God protect you, my child. These days men have gone crazy. They no longer know what they're doing."

They heard sounds in the street. Then someone knocked on the door. When Zahra opened the door, she saw several village women standing there, clothed in their black chadors. Among them were Sakineh, the wife of Massoud the barber; and Robabeh, the wife of Karim the sheep shearer.

"Ebrahim asked us to come over and stay with you. He's rounding up the men of the village. They're going to talk things over."

Zahra remained silent. She knew what that meant: the mayor had just called together his close advisers in order to come to a decision. All she said was: "Who is with him?"

"There's Mr. Lajevardi, Mr. Ramazani, Ghorban-Ali, and his two oldest sons, and there are also the kad-khoda's deputies, Shokrollah and Mohammad, and there's also Baba Koure, the old blind man who was drowsing down by the stream. I think that's all."

Islamic justice was in the process of being done, and nothing could stay its course. Nothing would be allowed to stand in its way, not even if a man were convinced of Soraya's innocence and should stand up and say it.

Zahra had no idea what might really be in store for Soraya as a result of their deliberations. As far back as she could remember, the decisions of the kadkhoda had never exceeded a fine, a pro forma sentence in order to set an example, or in some cases his requiring the accused or the culprit to make a donation to the community.

Rumors began to circulate, uncontrollable rumors. Messengers knocked at Zahra's door and spoke of grave decisions being made, of exemplary punishment. Men were gathered in front of the low-lying house that served as the town hall. Everyone had his opinion on the matter, as a result of which the market stalls were deserted, the shops empty, as all the male villagers met on the square to argue and discuss.

Zahra Khanum sent one of the women out to mix with the crowd. When the woman returned, she reported that the population was demanding the death penalty. As soon as she heard this, Zahra removed Soraya from the presence of the other women and closeted herself with her niece in the bedroom. She had very little time to forewarn her about what was happening and about the possibility of a heavy sentence. Later on, Zahra Khanum never said what Soraya's reaction had been and what had happened in the bedroom when the kadkhoda had come in person to announce the tribunal's decision. The only thing she said was that the young woman had seemed at peace with herself, that Soraya had not tried to justify or exonerate herself.

"I knew she was innocent of the crime she was accused of," Zahra said. "She had no need to tell me. Everyone here knew it as well, but nothing could stop that diabolical machine that the men of the village had set in motion."

When people later asked Zahra why she had given the young woman her most beautiful white dress, which she had kept neatly folded in the closet for decades, she simply said: "That morning Soraya had put on very simple clothes, to do her marketing. Convinced that once they had passed sentence they would not allow her to go back to her house, I wanted her to appear with proper dignity before her accusers. No one but me had ever worn that dress, not even my daughters on their wedding day. You have to admit that these were rather extraordinary circumstances!"

The women in their black chadors began to weep and pray. They always joined forces for funerals and were in the habit of psalmodizing together.

As the day wore on, the men's anger increased. Early in the afternoon the village resounded anew with hostile cries: "The woman's a bitch!" "Shameless one!" "A woman beyond redemption!" A little later one could hear other cries: "Let her be put to death!" "Death by stoning!" A few stones were thrown in the direction of Zahra's house; then there was silence, which lasted for only a few seconds. Next came a knock on the door. One of the women inside went to open it. Standing there were Maryam, the wife of the well digger Said, and Akram, the wife of the butcher Mehdi.

"The men have finished."

And with those words they departed.

5

T HE WOODEN DOOR opened.

A long murmur rose from the crowd. Here and there a few hostile cries rang out, muffled by a loud salvo of applause. Virtually everyone in Kupayeh was there spontaneously, having left behind their houses and shops to await the news. For almost an hour, beneath a sweltering sun, the villagers had commented about the morning's events among themselves.

The kadkhoda appeared. Then Sheik Hassan and a short, badly dressed man bent with age who was leaning on a cane, his wrinkled face set off by a full, white beard. As they reached the bottom step, Ebrahim and Hassan turned around and looked back respectfully at the third man.

In a voice that quivered slightly, the old man said "*Mahkum!*"

There was a huge roar from the crowd, and even the sound of a gun being fired. The dogs of the village, frightened by all the noise, began to bark. Arms were raised in a sign of fervor. Men applauded.

"Guilty! . . . She is guilty!"

The shouts increased mightily as the old man painfully descended the steps that separated him from the mayor and the mullah. Both of them helped him down, and the crowd moved aside to let him pass. Morteza had just condemned his own daughter, Soraya, to death.

Again silence fell over the crowd. A fourth person had just appeared in the doorway. It was Ghorban-Ali. He raised his right hand slowly and, in a solemn voice, intoned: *"Sang sâr*, let her be stoned!"

At that point the crowd became completely hysterical; insults spread like fire, and people began to dance.

Ghorban-Ali, as if caught up in the collective madness, screamed again at the top of his lungs: "Sang sâr!"

To which the crowd responded: "Stoned! Stoned! Let her be stoned!"

Ghorban-Ali had just sentenced his wife to death by stoning. He seemed radiant. Smiling broadly, almost jovial, he slowly descended the three steps that separated him from the crowd. Men slapped him affectionately and heartily on the back; others hugged him; children grabbed hold of his shirt. Arms seized him and lifted him off the ground.

The festivities could now begin, and the ritual run its course.

No one even paid any attention to the other men who emerged from the red-brick building, Ghorban-Ali's two oldest sons, both rough-hewn, strapping young men who were sixteen and eighteen years old, respectively; the mayor's two deputies; and the blind old man whom they guided slowly through the seething mob.

"Revenge by blood! Revenge by blood! Revenge by blood!"

The strange procession slowly wound its way down the village street and stopped in front of the fountain.

81

The sun was beating down, and an odor of sweat and dust floated in the air.

The men, shaggy and unkempt; the women, shrouded in their chadors; the excited children — all surrounded the nine men who had just rendered their verdict.

Machdi Ebrahim called for silence. The heat was so unbearable that it was hard to breathe. "Silence, please. Silence. May I please have your attention?"

Three times the kadkhoda had to repeat himself before the mob complied with his request.

"My friends, we are gathered here in front of the house of our dearly beloved Morteza Ramazani, the saddest, most humiliated, and loneliest man on the face of the earth today."

An angry murmur rose from the crowd. "True. How true that is. You're right. . . . Poor man!"

Again Ebrahim called for silence.

"Listen to me. . . . I beg of you. . . . Please listen to what I have to say."

Finally the crowd grew quiet again.

"Morteza Ramazani has been our friend and neighbor for lo, these many years. His father and his grandfather were born here. His children and his grandchildren were born here. His whole family is buried here, and never have any of its members left the village."

The crowd resumed its chant: "True. . . . Yes, all that is true."

Machdi Ebrahim raised his arm again: "The honor of our friend Morteza has been sullied. Not only that, but the honor of the village has also been tarnished, as has that of our families."

Again the assembly intoned, the chant this time

pierced by shouts and angry screams: "True! . . . True! . . . True!"

When the crowd grew quiet again, the kadkhoda went on: "But that is not all. There is something even worse. Morteza Ramazani's honor concerns only him and his family. The honor of our families concerns only us, and we know that it can be recovered. But I say to you, there is something far worse: the honor of God himself has been flouted, and the honor of the imam."

A pandemonium of shouts filled the air — two hundred and fifty strong — the women sobbing, the men roaring, the children beating their breasts in a sign of penitence. Sighs and moans and hostile shouts filled the air. "The whore has to die. . . . Death . . . death to the woman."

Once more Machdi Ebrahim called for silence. At first he could not make himself heard over the din of the excited crowd, which by now was almost out of control, but after several attempts he finally succeeded.

"It is in this house, a house all of us know, that Morteza Ramazani and all his family live. It is in this house that he was born many, many years ago, and it was in this house that he grew up with his family, in the respect and honor of God — "

The crowd broke in: "Praise be to God, the Compassionate, the Merciful. "

"It is therefore before this house, which we respect so highly, that we are going to read the verdict that we have reached, a verdict that will give back to Morteza and his family the honor they so rightly deserve."

"The verdict! . . . The verdict! . . . Read us the verdict!"

The expressions on the men's faces were filled with hate, and a few fists were thrown into the air. The women drew their veils more tightly around themselves, as if, all of a sudden, collective shame had rained down upon them.

"Let her be put to death . . . to death . . . to death. Now. Right here and now!"

Again Ebrahim called for silence. "My friends, I understand how you feel. But it is imperative that everything be accomplished in strict accordance with the laws of the country and of the edicts set forth by our venerable imam."

"He's right. . . . The man is right!" screamed the mob, its fury now completely unleashed. "The woman cannot be allowed to live. Let her be put to death, and put to death right now!"

Machdi was no longer able to control the villagers. Looking out at them, their faces deformed by intense emotion, he had trouble recognizing them. Could these be the same people who that morning had awakened at the first light of dawn, since it was market day? Right in front of him, scarcely three feet away, Mehdi the butcher, his wife's cousin, a man normally so mild-mannered and lighthearted, acted like someone possessed. Standing next to him, Rassoul the carpenter was gesticulating wildly and screaming that the guilty party had to be executed immediately, since he had work to finish before nightfall.

"My friends, by the grace of Almighty God, listen to me."

But the shouts resumed, louder and also more threatening than before.

84

"My children . . . my children."

Finally the crowd fell silent. The mayor knew that he had to act fast, for at any moment one of several trouble-makers was capable of leading the crowd to the house where Soraya was, a house guarded by only a handful of women.

"Listen to me, I beg you to hear what I have to say."

From an old, tattered eyeglass case, Machdi Ebrahim had taken a pair of round glasses with flexible rims, one of which was held in place by a piece of adhesive tape. He wiped the sweat from his brow with one of his hands. His other hand was trembling slightly but visibly.

"Let me read."

At those words the crowd fell suddenly silent. Flank-ing him on either side were Sheik Hassan and Morteza Ramazani, both of whom stood up a little straighter as Machdi Ebrahim began to speak. A foul-smelling, ochre-colored dust hung in the air, which was uncommonly still: not a breath of cooler air from the mountain slopes to offset the withering heat. Even the thin stream of water in the fountain seemed to have grown still.

"In the name of God, the Compassionate, the Merciful."

And the villagers responded in chorus: "Praise be to thee, oh Lord, All-powerful and just, praise be to thee."

"Today, the sixth day of Mordad in the year 1365,* the municipal council of Kupayeh has met in plenary

---

*The Muslim calendar dates from the voyage of Mohammad from Mecca to Medina in A.D. 622. Thus, to the year cited by Machdi Ebrahim, one must add 621 to get the Christian equivalent — 1986. The specific date was August 15, 1986.

session, with me presiding, and in the presence of my two deputies, Shokrollah Jalili and Mohammad Ghorbani.

"The meeting lasted for forty minutes. The decision taken was unanimous. Each member of the municipal council had an opportunity to voice his opinion. Not one member tried to defend the accused. We have all decided that the guilty party, Soraya Manutchehri — "

"Dishonor to her name. Dishonor to her name!"

Again shouts filled the air; some in the crowd began to push and shove; several women moaned; children burst out crying.

"Do not even speak her name any more! . . . Death to the harlot! . . . Let it be over and done with now . . . without wasting another minute!"

A stone thrown by someone in the crowd struck Morteza Ramazani directly in the chest. He slumped slowly to the ground, and the mob fell silent once again.

"Who dared to strike this man? Whoever threw that stone, step forward and make yourself known. Who threw that stone?"

The crowd, ashamed at what had happened, lowered its head as if in chorus. Some people helped the old man over to the fountain and propped him up against it. Someone brought him a pillow so he could rest his head on the edge of the basin.

"It's all right," he murmured. "Just a slight pain here, on the right. . . . It's nothing. . . . Go on . . . don't worry about me."

The mayor, who had been kneeling down beside the wounded man, slowly got to his feet and, pointing a finger at the now silent villagers, said: "You have wounded our friend for the second time in the space of a few hours. God will not forgive you. Even as he was being humiliated by his daughter, you struck him again this afternoon. What has he done to deserve such a fate, this good and decent man whose door is always open to all of us?"

Just then Sheik Hassan spoke up for the first time. Up to this point he had said nothing, preferring to listen to the mayor and to the shouts and imprecations of the villagers under his jurisdiction. He pointed his forefinger toward the crowd, specifically in the direction of a group that was especially worked up. "You over there . . . yes, you in the black shirt. Come over here."

The crowd opened up a path.

"Come here . . . and hurry up!"

A young man of about fifteen walked slowly over toward the mullah, whose arm was still raised, pointing in his direction.

"You're the son of Yadollah the shepherd, isn't that right?"

The young man was slow to respond.

"Answer me: are you the son of Yadollah the shepherd?"

"Yes," the boy said in a muffled voice as he bowed his head.

"Why did you throw that stone at Morteza Ramazani?"

After a second's hesitation, the boy replied: "It wasn't me. . . . I swear it wasn't me."

Even before he could finish his sentence, the bejeweled hand of the cleric descended on the boy's cheek with a resounding slap. The adolescent fell backward and sprawled in the dust. People picked him up. A thin stream of blood flowed from his mouth.

"Not only are you hard of heart, but you're a liar as well! I'm ashamed for you and for your family. Luckily your father wasn't here to witness this. If he had been, he would have hit you a lot harder than I just did."

Then, regaining his composure, the mullah went on: "Why did you throw that stone?"

"It wasn't me. . . . I wasn't the only one. . . . Ali and Rahim threw stones, too. It's not me."

Again a blow, just as violent as the first, struck the boy; his lip burst open and blood spurted out.

"Please don't . . . please don't hit me again! Yes, I'm the one who threw the stone. . . . Please forgive me."

The boy was dragged beyond the perimeter of the crowd and tossed onto a pile of manure, on which hundreds of flies were swarming.

The mayor, who had remained completely impassive throughout the event, resumed his reading: "We have unanimously decided that the guilty party, Soraya Man-utchehri, shall be stoned before the day ends, until she is dead."

An even louder clamor of hostile shouts and cries of joy greeted the mayor's announcement. "Death to the whore. . . . Death to the prostitute."

Once again Machdi Ebrahim called for silence. "There is no point in shouting. Everything shall be done in strict accordance with the law, as the Koran authorizes us in cases such as this, and as the law requires. God, the All-powerful, orders us to make sure that we ourselves see that justice is done, for we have all been sullied by this woman and because her family demands revenge."

"Revenge! . . . Revenge! . . . God demands justice and revenge!"

"My friends, listen to me! Please, I beg you to listen to what I have to say. You will have your revenge, each and every one of you, when the time has come, but I repeat to you that all shall be done in accordance with the will of God and according to the desires of our greatly revered imam."

Ebrahim removed his glasses, carefully put them back into their battered case, and went on: "There has never been a case of stoning in our village before. Here our citizens have always led decent and honorable lives. But I do know that last year a woman was stoned to death not far from here, in Khajeh Asghar, and the year before at Shahre Babak. One of my friends from Kerman has described to me how it was done. We will proceed in the same way."

"Now," a man in the first row shouted. "Let's do it right away!"

"He's right," another man echoed. "Let's do it right away."

"The ceremony will take place on the town square," Machdi Ebrahim said, "in one hour's time, so that everyone can be present. Meanwhile, I have to go and read the sentence to Soraya."

"You don't have to do that," cried a one-eyed man, who was already holding a stone in one hand. "Let's go and get her right now. We don't have any time to waste. I'm ready. I'll throw the first stone myself. That's all it will take. That's the way I kill rabbits, with one stone."

"We shall proceed in the way I just described," Machdi Ebrahim replied, "the way God asks that it be done, the way our respected imam authorizes us to proceed, and as Morteza desires. Now, all of you, calm down and go back home. In one hour Soraya will be taken to the town square. For the time being, go back to your work. I don't want any of you to show your faces till the appointed hour. Then, and only then, will you come to the square."

Slowly the crowd began to break up. The women returned home; the men went back to their shops; and the children headed off to play in the fields.

Now Machdi Ebrahim and Sheik Hassan had the task of officially informing Soraya that she had only a short time to live. Everyone in the village already knew it, except for the women keeping watch in Zahra's house.

It was the first time in the history of the village that the mayor had to carry out such a mission. He felt proud of the charge but also uneasy. He knew that since the revolution had triumphed in the country, the tribunals had sent thousands of people to be executed. He listened to the official radio twice a day and heard the names of those who had committed sins against God and the imam. He knew that down in Kerman the revolutionary tribunals had been working around the clock for the past six years, meting out sentences. But never before had he voted to send someone to her death. Never before had he organized an execution.

6

AN HOUR HAD PASSED since the men had emerged from the town hall to announce their verdict.

Outside, everything was quiet. The sun began to descend, and the square that Machdi Ebrahim and Sheik Hassan had just left was freshened by a slight breeze.

In the front room of Zahra's house, the mourners had resumed their lamentations, which were interrupted now and then by some verses from the Koran.

In the bedroom behind, Zahra leaned down over Soraya and murmured to her: "My sweet Soraya, know that I will be next to you no matter what happens, and no matter what happens my affection and esteem will be with you. But what more can I do? This is the law of men, the law that men make and say it is the law of God. They have found you guilty, whereas you are not. They have sentenced you, whereas you are innocent, but no one can prove it, not you, not me, not the good women in the next room."

Soraya understood for the first time how much the silence into which she had withdrawn over the past few months had worked against her. All of a sudden she was seized with the overwhelming desire to speak up, to explain, to justify, to proclaim her innocence to high heaven. But she knew that it was too late, and that no one among those who had tried and sentenced her would believe her. Yet she still found it hard to imagine that this gross, all-too-obvious plot could actually result in her death.

She felt the urgent need to tell Aunt Zahra everything she was feeling and thinking. "Aunt Zahra, I'm not afraid of death. I've already been dead for some time now, since my mother died, since Ghorban-Ali started to humiliate me, to hit me, since he left me and took up with other women."

She couldn't go on; she was sobbing too hard. She felt herself growing faint, slipping to the floor. Zahra knelt down beside her, took Soraya's head in her arms, kissed her on the forehead: "My child . . . my poor dear child . . . don't be ashamed to cry. Cry as long and as hard as you want. There's no one here to hear you, no one to see you . . . let yourself go. Cry, my child, cry."

Next door, the women's mourning grew louder: "Oh God, the All-powerful . . . oh Mohammad . . . oh God, the Beloved . . . oh merciful Prophet . . ."

"Aunt Zahra, I don't want to leave you; I don't want to leave my children, my little Khojasteh who isn't even seven. . . . I don't want to leave this life, and yet I'm not afraid, for I know that where I'm going Mama will be there, and I miss her so. Aunt Zahra, take care of my children for me, especially the little one, she's so delicate, and her health isn't all that good."

She was sobbing harder now, and her words were stifled by short, little gasps. "Aunt Zahra, promise me that one day when she's older you'll tell her about me, who I really was and what they did to me, so she won't be ashamed of her mother. Promise me you'll do that."

Deeply touched, the old woman replied: "My dear

child, your children, especially the youngest ones, will live with me and will always have everything they need. Your children will be my children, and no one will ever take them away from me. My home will be their home."

In saying those words, Zahra knew that her promise did not include Soraya's oldest sons. Both boys were following in their father's footsteps and, with his blessing, were indulging in all sorts of petty trafficking and dubious schemes.

Hussein-Ali, the older boy, was the spitting image of his father: same square face, deep-set eyes, the same kind of scraggly beard and mustache, and a heavyset neck impressive for someone his age. He had attended school for all of three years, distinguishing himself only by his truancy and insubordination.

While he was still quite young, he attracted attention by his bad habits: breaking windows; pilfering; stealing chickens and rabbits, whose throats he would then slit before heading off into the mountains to build a fire and roast them. He also stood out because of his endless fights with the other boys his age.

At first his father admonished him, sometimes beating him for his misdemeanors — in fact, he still had a nasty scar behind his right ear where his father had once hit him. But the more he was beaten, the more he tended to relapse into the same pattern of petty crime. Tough, ill-tempered, and violent, he divided his time among the fields, the stables, the neighboring forests, and the family household, to which he repaired only to eat and sleep.

Hassan-Ali, his younger brother by two years, was physically his opposite. Lighter-skinned, he had finer features and high cheekbones. He was a good student, even tempered, and affectionate. Always obliging and ready to be of service, he helped both his mother and the neighbors carry their groceries, fill up their pails at the well, bring in the cattle, or milk the cows. But when the only classroom in the village was closed down and the students sent home, Hassan-Ali was left to his own devices and to the nefarious influence of his older brother. He didn't steal, but he was a passive participant in his brother's operations, a silent and slightly bemused accomplice.

When they were asked to be present at the father's trial of their mother, they found that to be quite natural, and when the assembled men were asked if they found Soraya guilty, the two boys raised their hands with the rest of the self-constituted all-male tribunal.

Zahra Khanum was seated next to her niece. She was leaning slightly forward, praying. Her lips moved, but it was almost impossible to hear her words. She was staring fixedly at Soraya, who had turned so white that all of a sudden Zahra was afraid. She interrupted her litanies and asked, "Soraya . . . Soraya . . . can you hear me?"

Her niece, who seemed to be in another world, did not respond.

"Soraya, my child . . . can you hear me?"

The young woman looked at her aunt, impassive, absent.

Zahra reached out and laid her hand on Soraya's shoulder.

"Answer me. . . . Do you hear me?"

94

Only then did the young woman lower her eyes, and two tears coursed down her cheeks.

Zahra hugged Soraya in her arms, in defiance of all local conventions, which strictly forbade anyone from touching someone who had been tried and sentenced, no matter what the punishment had been.

"Aunt Zahra, I saw my mother. She was sitting under a tree, and she reached out her arms to me. She smiled at me and said: 'At last, my child, at long last you've come. It took you so long, so very long to come.' " Her sobs became more violent, so much so that the mourners in the next room paused for a moment in their lamentations.

There was a knock on the window, then another. They could hear a voice: "Zahra Khanum, the hour has come. Machdi Ebrahim has told me to come and let you know. . . . You must come now."

Zahra was the first to rise, then she helped her niece to her feet. Behind them, on the threshold of the next room, five shadows dressed in black awaited them, still murmuring their prayers. Once again there was a knock on the window, this time a little more insistent.

"Zahra Khanum, did you hear me? . . . The time has come. . . . People are waiting."

The old woman took Soraya by the arm and walked with her toward the door; the other women followed close behind. Zahra and Soraya looked at each other.

As Zahra started to open the front door to her house, she whispered to Soraya: "Courage, my child. You are innocent, and God knows it. . . . He knows it full well."

Carefully, cautiously, she opened the door and was immediately struck, as though it were a slap in the face, by a blast of burning air in a setting of utter silence. Zahra crossed the threshold first. Her head was covered with her chador, but her face was visible. Her deep wrinkles and leathered face gave her the look of a witch. She both frightened people and inspired respect.

Five hundred eyes were fixed upon her.

And suddenly all hell broke loose: people began to push and shove, to shout and scream. Fists shot into the air. Soraya had just appeared in Zahra's wake, clothed in her chador, her face completely veiled. The seven dark silhouettes stood there motionless in the hot, humid air of that summer afternoon. Six uncovered faces and one completely veiled were waiting, as if rooted to the spot, for Machdi Ebrahim, who was in charge of the events of that extraordinary day, to decide what would happen next.

As quickly as the shouts of the crowd had erupted, they suddenly ceased as the mayor, who had climbed up on a stepladder, began to speak: "The hour has come. . . . The sentence must be carried out!"

A murmur coursed through the crowd. Then one strident voice rose above the others: "Now . . . right now."

And as if in echo, another responded: "Yes, let it be carried out now."

And still another: "He's right. This has gone on long enough. Let it be done and done quickly!"

Ebrahim raised his right arm and waited for the noise to subside: "This has been a long and difficult day, and it is not over yet. As I have said, we intend to proceed according to the rules of law. Mr. Lajevardi, who is here beside me, insists that everything be carried out in accordance with the constitution of our country and with the laws of Islam."

Then, turning to Zahra Khanum, he said with great show: "Bring forth the guilty party, if you please."

The old woman hesitated for a brief moment, turned toward Soraya, and said softly: "Be strong . . . look straight ahead . . . lift your head and hold it high, for you are innocent."

The two women, followed by the five mourners, began to make their way through the crowd, which parted to let them pass. There was total silence.

Then, all of a sudden, people began to spit, to scream insults at the condemned woman, to strike her with their hands or fists as she passed by. Not only Soraya but also the mourners behind her were struck by the blows. Only Zahra was spared.

From his perch atop the stepladder, Machdi Ebrahim saw everything that was happening, but he did nothing to stop it. He knew that would be pointless. The crowd had been waiting so long, it had the right to vent its anger.

Then suddenly a fist struck Zahra on the back of the neck. She stopped in her tracks, raised her head, and stared at the attacker: "You bastard!" she said. "Here, I have something for you!"

And with that she administered a resounding blow to the offender.

The crowd tittered, and for a brief moment everyone seemed to relax ever so slightly. Then the procession moved on toward the center of the square. Soraya was walking so close behind the old woman that they seemed almost to be glued together.

Those in the rear, the five mourners, had resumed their incantations and chants: "All-powerful God . . . forgive us our sins. . . . Oh Mohammad, have pity on us."

The fatal cortege stopped in front of the stepladder. With the help of Sheik Hassan, Machdi Ebrahim climbed down from the ladder. A circle formed around the women and the Islamic judges. Everyone wanted to see, and hear with their own ears, exactly what was going to happen now, what the young woman who was destined to be put to death within the half hour was going to say.

With a slow, emphatic gesture of his hand, the mayor waved the women clad in black to step back, so that Soraya could be alone to face her executioners. It was as if, in the space of a few hours, this colorless character, the mayor, had become a different man. One had the impression that he was standing taller, that he no longer needed his cane to walk. Sheik Hassan was neatly trimmed; he had felt compelled to pay a visit to the barber before the ceremony that was about to take place. Only Morteza, the injured father, betrayed his state of distress by the unaccustomed disarray of his clothing.

Again the crowd began to grow restless: "Kill her. . . . Let her be put to death."

Ebrahim made no effort to calm the villagers down. Hostile cries served to increase the tension; nothing better for an execution. He wanted the event to be engraved in the minds of the villagers, never to be forgotten, as he wanted the echoes of the sentence handed down by God to be heard down in the valley, throughout the whole province. And, who knows, the news might even travel as far as the capital.

And what if the imam himself were to hear of this ceremony, this sacrifice carried out in his name? What an honor that would be!

Therefore, it was essential that everything be done in strict accordance with the rules.

"Soraya Manutchehri, after fair and honest deliberation we have reached a verdict. You are aware what that verdict is."

"Death! . . . Death! . . . Death!"

"Did you hear what they said? Our country's justice has determined that you should be put to death."

"Now! . . . Now! . . . Move aside and let's get started!"

One could see that the men were already armed with stones, with clubs, even with various kinds of tools. The crowd was almost out of control. People began whistling, and the mayor could tell that the laughter was hostile and more and more menacing. He knew that he had better move fast or else the crowd, led by some of the angrier men who were literally out of control, would take matters into its own hands.

"As I've already told you, everything has to take place legally, and Mr. Lajevardi, who is here beside me, will make sure the sentence is carried out properly, so that no one can ever reproach us for having acted outside the law of God and of the will of our beloved imam."

"Praise be to God, and to the imam. Long live the imam. . . . May God protect our guide."

The crowd seemed to settle down a bit. But it would

have taken only one inflammatory word or gesture to set it off again. At a glance from the mayor, Sheik Hassan began to speak: "My friends, you know me well now. I haven't lived very long here in this beautiful village, but Almighty God has dispatched me to be among you, and I shall never leave Kupayeh, which for me is a paradise on earth."

His words were greeted by scattered applause. Hassan had understood that he needed to flatter these rough, illiterate people if he wanted to make sure the ceremony would be carried out the way he desired.

These peasants were coming to a stoning the same way they would have gathered to see an ayatollah or, in earlier times, a prince of the former regime. It was a spectacle, an entertainment. Once the show was over, they would all go back to their daily chores and labors.

Only the elders of the village, sitting around the fire in the evening, would discuss and comment on the event, commiserating with one another.

"This woman" — the mullah pointed a threatening finger at Soraya — "has defiled our village, and this blemish on our honor demands atonement. You, the people of this village, will obtain the required redress by applying the word of God."

"Sang sâr! Sang sâr. Let her be stoned."

"Yes, my friends, you are right. Each of you in turn will have a chance to cleanse the offense by throwing a stone at her, but it must be an orderly process, as laid down by the law. At each stone thrown, your honor will be restored to you in some degree, until she has atoned for her sin."

"Sang sâr! Sang sâr!"

Sheik Hassan resumed: "Go now and find yourselves some stones. Go, and be back here as soon as you can. . . . We won't begin until you all have your stones."

Several dozen men dispersed to the four corners of the village to look for weapons of death. They plucked stones out of the stream; they took bricks out of the ruins of a wall, tiles from a roof that had collapsed. Those who were watching could even see half a dozen men demolishing the wall of a small house that was under construction, to make sure they did not come back empty-handed!

In less than ten minutes the circle had re-formed. Zahra Khanum and the women mourners were still in the first row, as were Ghorban-Ali and his two oldest sons, Hussein-Ali and Hassan-Ali; Ebrahim's two deputies, Shokrollah Jalili and Mohammed Ghorbani; and the blind old man.

Standing in front of them, still veiled, Soraya Manutchehri knew that the die had been cast, that it was all over. She stood absolutely still. She was less than three feet away from the kadkhoda, the mullah, and her father.

The ceremony could begin.

"Who has a pickax? Who has a stake?"

Machdi glanced about, looking for Rassoul the carpenter.

"I do," shouted a man from somewhere in the middle of the crowd.

"Me, too," screamed someone else.

Then there were shouts from others offering their services and tools.

"Come here," the mayor ordered, "come over here next to me."

A half dozen of the villagers joined the circle, which was forced to spread out to let the newcomers in. The delighted volunteers took up a position to the rear of Soraya. They were all carrying their tools in one hand and a stone in the other. In addition to Rassoul the carpenter, there were Majid and Moshen, the sons of the village butcher; Asghar, Rahmatollah, and Ali-Akbar, all of whom were Ghorban-Ali's cousins. These last three were always ready to lend a helping hand for any heavy work that needed to be done in the village. Whenever a truck would arrive in town — which wasn't often — bringing in tanks of bottled gas, drums of oil, huge sacks of rice or bags of cement, they were always there to help unload the supplies; whenever a flash flood would wash away the little bridge over the stream, they immediately went out to rebuild it; they chopped down trees; they carried stones to building sites; they slaughtered lambs for sacrificial occasions.

"You are all volunteering for the task?"

"Yes," they responded as one.

Ebrahim pointed to Rassoul and his pickax. "Come . . . follow me. Step back there, you people."

The circle of villagers opened up to allow the mayor and his gravediggers through. Meanwhile, the woman accused of adultery was still standing there like a black-clad statue.

Machdi Ebrahim pointed to a spot on the far side of the square, exactly where the bus from Kerman stopped. The ground there was hard and rocky. Here and there a few weeds grew, and scorpions were sleeping in the sun.

"There," Machdi said to Rassoul. "That's where you should dig. The carpenter spit on the palms of both his hands, took hold of his pickax, and looked at the crowd. "In the name of Allah," he said loudly and took a stance with his feet planted wide apart. He raised the pick above his head and struck the ground with all his strength.

Twenty, thirty times he dug his pick into the ground, calling upon the name of God to give him courage.

Ten minutes later the hole was about a foot and a half deep. Rassoul straightened up for a moment to catch his breath and then swung the pickax once again. Ebrahim motioned for him to stop.

"That's enough for now. Good job. Let someone else take over."

Then, turning to the butcher's two sons, he said: "Who wants to take over?"

Moshen took the pick from his brother's hands and headed toward the hole. "Allah be praised!" he shouted as he started to dig.

The hole rapidly increased in size, and the color of the earth became darker the deeper they went. The mayor motioned again, and Moshen handed the pick to Majid, who kept digging as fast as his brother had. Within twenty minutes or so, the hole was a good three feet deep.

"All right, Asghar, your turn," the mayor said.

Asghar picked up a shovel, and when his stint was finished, the mayor called on Rassoul to take over again, then the two brothers. At this point the hole was almost four feet deep.

"Is that deep enough?" Majid asked.

"A little bit more. Another five or six inches. That ought to do it."

Asghar went to work again with his shovel, then passed it on to Rahmatollah, who in turn handed it to Ali-Akbar.

At last Machdi Ebrahim seemed satisfied.

"That's fine. You can put your tools away now. Follow me."

The mayor and his deputies returned to the circle of villagers, who had been following the proceedings in fascinated silence. The sun had moved closer to the horizon, and a bit of a breeze had come up, giving the men and women of Kupayeh the illusion that it was growing cooler.

During the entire time the hole was being dug, Sheik Hassan had remained impassive. Soraya was facing him, and from behind her black veil, which protected her, she watched him closely. Nonplussed, she stared at him with complete contempt. She simply could not understand how such an imposter could have brought her to this pass, have led her to the threshold of death. Ever since the day when, after having connived to obtain for himself the arbab's former house, the man had settled down in the village, the young woman had grown to know his true nature. Several times, taking advantage of his position as mullah — Soraya had never managed to believe in the sincerity of his declarations of faith — he had done his best to entice her into his house, during the empty hours of the afternoon when Ghorban-Ali was

104

away in the city and the rest of the village was out working in the fields. There were other times when, knowing she was alone, he had tried to get himself invited to her house in order, as he put it, to speak to her about God and about the role of women in the young republic. . . . Until that day when he had barged into her house uninvited, only to be sent packing by Zahra Khanum.

Standing there, holding the Koran in his hand, Sheik Hassan was also staring at Soraya from behind his dark glasses. He had not forgotten the indignities she had caused him by refusing his advances. She had dared to resist him, and she could see now what that kind of conduct led to! Yet at thirty-five — or maybe a trifle older — she was still a very beautiful woman. She knew she was about to be abandoned by her husband, who let it be known to anyone who cared to listen that he had every intention of marrying a girl from the city. Under those circumstances, what more could the woman dream of than taking up with him?

She had been stupid to turn him down; no doubt that old witch Zahra had had a negative influence on her.

Still, the rumor that Sheik Hassan had acted in some way offensive to the young woman had spread like wildfire through the village, carefully and artfully nurtured by Zahra Khanum. For a time, early on in his stay, the mullah was pointed at by the villagers, who openly avoided him. But Ghorban-Ali had turned things around by insinuating that Soraya was not a good woman and that, in fact, she had tried to lure poor Sheik Hassan into her trap in order to compromise him. And as quickly as she had been supported and pitied by the villagers, now it was she who was despised and avoided. Slowly but surely, her husband's snare tightened around her. Yet he needed to furnish further proof of his wife's misconduct. Firouzeh's death provided him with an unexpected, and unhoped-for, opportunity. Ghorban-Ali and the mullah were not unaware of the village gossip that was going around about Soraya's attraction to the widower — gossip they repeated and embroidered on until they had entrapped the poor woman in their carefully contrived plot. . . .

Sheik Hassan climbed up on the stepladder and said: "Now let us pray, let us render thanks to God and to our venerable imam."

"Yes," echoed the voices, "he is right . . . he is right, let us pray to God."

Hassan raised the Koran that he was holding in one hand and began: "In the Name of God, the Compassionate, the Merciful."

And the crowd, men and women alike, repeated together: "In the Name of God, the Compassionate, the Merciful."

Hassan went on, he and his deputies reciting in chorus: "Praise be to God, Master of the universe, the Merciful, the All-forgiving, he who reigns supreme at the day of retribution. It is you we adore, it is you whom we beg to come to our help. Direct us onto the path of righteousness, the path of those upon whom you have heaped rewards for their good deeds; keep us from the path of those who have earned thy wrath, and those who have strayed from the paths of righteousness."

106

Scarcely had these words been spoken than the throbbing of a motor could be heard. Suddenly, from around the last curve of the mountain road appeared two dusty, gaudily painted vehicles. Ebrahim looked at Hassan, who in turn looked over at Ghorban-Ali, who stared back at him. Who were these characters? Where in the world had they come from at this hour of the afternoon?

Out of the two cars climbed four people, all oddly dressed: bright-colored trousers; absurd-looking shirts; faces covered with greasepaint; all sporting beards, whether real or false; shaggy, unkempt hair. Following in their wake were two monkeys, a goat, and a dog.

"Good afternoon, ladies and gentlemen," said one of them, who seemed to be the leader. "We bring you greetings. My friends and I are honored to be here in this beautiful village of yours."

It was a group of itinerant performers, one of several hundred such troupes that toured the country from one end to the other. The man went on: "In the city, they told us that today was market day in your fair village. So we said to ourselves, let us hasten there, so that we can amuse and distract you after a hard day's work. . . . Come one, come all, and that includes the children, don't be afraid. . . . Come and see all the wonderful things we have in store for you."

And with that he flung a handful of confetti into the air, then another, then a third, which soared like so many pieces of sparkling lights into the turquoise sky.

"Catch," he shouted, this time addressing the children, "catch the candy if you can!" and he tossed a couple of dozen pieces of candy, all wrapped in brightly colored paper, which soared then fell onto the dusty square, as twenty or so children scrambled to pick them up.

The adult villagers were standing stock still, in total silence. Sheik Hassan was perched on his ladder, the holy book clutched in both his hands, flanked by Ebrahim and Morteza, with Soraya directly in front of him and the women mourners behind him. Not a soul moved.

"Finish your prayers. . . . Please excuse us . . . we didn't know . . . don't pay any attention to us. . . . We'll get ourselves set up, and when you've finished please do come and see us. There will be something for everyone: candy, toys, animals that will amaze you with their performances, magic tricks such as you have never seen before, all sorts of things for young and old alike. . . . But as I said, only when you've finished your prayers. Meanwhile, don't pay us any mind."

A slight sense of uneasiness had come over the crowd; then Machdi Ebrahim began to speak: "We have a task to complete. Everyone, come on back here. . . . That includes you children over there; you can go and visit these gentlemen later on, when we've finished."

The tension had lessened a notch or two, and both the mayor and the mullah were perfectly aware that the crowd had lost its concentration. Sheik Hassan climbed down off the stepladder, adjusted his turban, and announced: "With the permission of his honor the mayor, let us begin."

Machdi Ebrahim motioned to Zahra Khanum and asked her to come forward. Then, leaning over toward her, he said: "Take the condemned woman by the arm and follow me. Tell the other women to come, too."

108

Then, making his way slowly, and flanked by the mullah and the accused adulteress's father, he began walking toward the gaping hole that had been dug on the far side of the square, near the spot where the itinerant troupe had just pulled up and parked. It was a good hundred and fifty feet away.

The strolling players had not yet noticed anything out of the ordinary. A mullah on a stepladder, the villagers gathered to recite their prayers, the hole a short distance from their cars, had not struck them as all that unusual. Traveling from one corner to the other of the country, they had seen many things in their time, things far stranger than this scene. But they were clearly not prepared for what now seemed to be happening, especially the slow, inexorable advance of the villagers toward them, stones and pickaxes and clubs in their hands, chanting the verses of the Koran.

The man who appeared to be the group's leader straightened up and called out to his companions: "Hey! Look! . . . Look at that. . . . They're coming toward us!"

The man wiped his brow and stammered: "Gentlemen . . . gentlemen . . . what, ah, what exactly is going on? What do you want us to do? You want us to leave? Just tell us what you want, and we'll be happy to oblige."

Ebrahim, Hassan, and Morteza advanced without replying, with two hundred and fifty fierce-looking people following close behind. The kadkhoda stopped a few steps from the troupe: "I want you to move away from here. Take your cars, and park them somewhere else. And be quick about it. Can't you see we're in the middle of something here? Now do as I say. And get a move on you!"

"Yes, sir, right away. This minute. . . . But what is going on?"

"You'll soon see. . . . Now go! In the name of Allah! Take everything you have with you. See those trees down there? Go park yourselves under those trees. You can look on if you like, but above all stay put!"

The visitors did not need to be asked twice. They backed up the vehicles about thirty yards or so and took all the animals and equipment with them as well.

Then Ebrahim turned around: "Zahra, bring the guilty woman over here."

The crowd slowly stepped back as the women appeared. It was only then that the traveling troupe discovered what was taking place: coming toward them were half a dozen women, all clothed in their black chadors, one of whom was completely veiled, and dozens of men armed with stones and bricks. Terrified, they all took several steps back. They were tempted to decamp, but held their ground, as if paralyzed with surprise and amazement. They stayed where they were, making sure to keep a safe distance from the villagers. Zahra and Soraya had reached a point about thirty feet from the hole. Machdi Ebrahim motioned for them to stop.

"That will do. . . . Now, turn around; face us so that everyone can see you."

The two women turned around. In the front row of the crowd were the mullah, Soraya's father, her husband, her two oldest sons, the mayor's deputies, and the old blind man, who always followed in the others' wake, and in whose hand they had also placed a stone.

An impressive silence fell over the square.

"Zahra Khanum, remove the condemned woman's veil."

Slowly, very slowly, the old woman did as she was bid. She let go of poor Soraya's arm, came around in front of her, and removed the veil that had been protecting her face from the villagers' stares.

Soraya's eyes were closed. The chador that covered her head made her face look infinitely paler than it really was. Her lips were pressed tightly together, and her mouth was quivering ever so slightly.

The crowd suddenly resumed its rain of invectives. "Whore! . . . Fallen woman! . . . Shameless harlot! . . . Bitch . . . let the bitch be put to death! . . . Death to the whore!"

Arms were raised, ready to let loose a barrage of stones and bricks. Machdi Ebrahim placed himself between the two women and the villagers.

"My friends, the time has come. . . . The sentence must be carried out. . . . God has commanded us to do so."

"We've waited long enough," one voice screamed out.

"He's right. This has gone on long enough. Let's get it over with and get back to our work," another shouted.

"Death to the bitch! Now! Not later, now!"

The mayor raised his hand.

"All will be done as God has decided. Nothing will be changed. You must be patient."

The stepladder was brought to him and he climbed up with considerable difficulty.

"Our deeply respected Morteza Ramazani will throw

111

the first stone. If he misses the mark, he will be given a second stone. In fact, he will be given as many stones as it takes for him to hit the guilty one. Then it will be Ghorban-Ali's turn."

"That's only fair," someone called out. "Long live Morteza!"

"Then it will be Hassan Lajevardi's turn, as God's representative among us and as our imam in this village."

"Praise be to God. . . . Long life to our imam . . . long live Mr. Lajevardi!" other voices called out, more and more heated.

"After that the condemned woman's sons will have their turn, our dear Hussein-Ali and Hassan-Ali, who since this morning have been suffering greatly. By this gesture shall their honor be restored to them."

Then, looking around at the circle of villagers who had again fallen silent, he said: "Finally, it will be the turn of our little community. All of you will have the right to throw a stone at this unworthy woman who has by her actions defiled all of us."

Cries of joy filled the air, louder than ever; arms shot up threateningly, and the crowd took several steps forward.

Machdi Ebrahim climbed down from his perch and once again spoke to Zahra: "Zahra Khanum, be good enough to remove the condemned party's chador."

The old woman knew, from that moment on, that the die had been irrevocably cast. Nothing could now stop the course of events. Slowly she opened the long black veil that shrouded Soraya, revealing her white dress. At that point old Morteza noticed that his daughter was wearing the necklace that he had given her on the seventh day after his wife, Shokat, had died. With great difficulty he straightened up and yelled hoarsely: "Take that off, vile daughter, take off that necklace . . . it belongs to your sainted mother. . . . Oh Lord God, how much suffering do I have to endure?" Then he collapsed on the ground.

Zahra Khanum removed the delicate gold necklace from the young woman's neck and handed it to the kadkhoda, who in turn gave it to the old man, who was slowly being helped to his feet. Regaining consciousness, Morteza deftly slipped the necklace into his pocket.

"Harlot! . . . Defiler of the family honor! . . . Wretched creature! . . . Return to dust from whence you came!"

Soraya was bareheaded. Her eyes were still closed. With infinite care, Zahra took her arm and led her, step by tiny step, toward the gaping hole.

"Pray, my child, pray with all your might, for God is waiting for you, and paradise is open unto you. Pray for us, too, for we know not what we do."

She felt like taking Soraya in her arms, but she did not have the strength. As she left the young woman, she squeezed her arm ever so slightly. The two women looked at each other for a fleeting moment. They had said their last good-byes.

"Zahra Khanum, come over here. Rejoin us," ordered the mayor.

Soraya turned her back to the crowd, which was silent now. Standing erect and motionless, she was no more than three feet from the hole. Her long hair cascaded

113

down across her shoulders, all the way to her waist.

At a command from Machdi Ebrahim, she turned around till she was facing the villagers, but this time her eyes were open. Without flinching, she studied the faces of those who were watching her. There were Shokrollah Jalili and Mohammad Ghorbani, the mayor's two deputies; Sheik Hassan, more arrogant than ever in his mullah's garb; her husband and their two sons, each of whom was holding two stones. Her gaze met that of her father, and for a fleeting second she thought she detected in his eyes a look of embarrassment, of uneasiness, for Morteza lowered his eyes when his daughter looked directly at him. Next to him, Machdi Ebrahim, tall and desiccated, was leaning on his cane; then there were Mehdi the butcher; Rassoul the carpenter; Massoud the barber; and all the other men. And then, finally, there was Aunt Zahra, a small figure almost lost among the mourners.

7

THE ITINERANT CLOWNS had moved a trifle closer, without making a sound. They had locked up their animals in the two old ramshackle vehicles and were watching the proceedings from a distance. Still made up and dressed in their grotesque costumes, they had inched forward a few steps in order not to miss any of the "spectacle."

During all their travels throughout the years, as they had gone from town to town and village to village, they had heard a thousand tales and gathered a thousand memories which they drew upon to nourish and enliven their performances. These tales and memories were like a chronicle of the places they had visited, one which changed in keeping with events and the passage of time, an oral fable, a grotesque caricature of daily life in the rural parts of the land. But never before in their travels had they witnessed an execution, much less a death by stoning. To be sure, during the past few years there had been a marked increase in the number of executions that had taken place in the four corners of the land. They had heard many stories about hangings, and about people being executed by firing squads. But this time they were going to be the startled witnesses of an event that, from that day forward, they would always talk about, and on which they would embroider to their heart's content, to the extent that what they had seen had terrified them.

At a gesture from Machdi Ebrahim, Shokrollah and Mohammad stepped forth from the first row of villagers.

The woman who had been sentenced to death stood facing the silent crowd. Her head was held high, and her eyes were glued to old Zahra, who was staring back at her.

At another sign from the mayor, the two men took Soraya under her arms, lifted her up, and deposited her in the hole.

A murmur ran through the crowd. This time the performance was really going to begin. That was what had brought them here, and they were growing more and more restive and increasingly excited as they looked at the defenseless woman being lowered into the pit. Stone in hand, they awaited Machdi Ebrahim's orders.

The gravediggers returned with their shovels and spades and began to fill up the hole. With each shovelful of dirt, they intoned "In the name of Allah!" to give themselves courage.

Zahra Khanum noted that the men went about their task with a kind of respect and professional conscience. No rough movements, no violence, nothing hurried. They were extremely careful not to soil Soraya's white dress unnecessarily, and especially not to hurt her in any way. The kadkhoda raised his hand, and the men put down their tools.

Soraya was buried up to her shoulders, her arms entombed in the soil, her long hair spread out around her. She appeared completely absent: she looked around without seeing, listened without hearing the nearby voices.

Machdi Ebrahim had resumed speaking: "Soraya Manutchehri, the moment has come when the judgment of God is to be carried out, when you will be made to pay for your sins. Do you have something to say? Is there anything you want to tell us?"

The condemned woman did not respond. She was not even looking at the mayor; she was staring vacantly into space; she was dazed, completely lost in her own thoughts.

"If you have something to say," the mayor went on, "now is the time to say it. . . . Afterward, it will be too late."

The silence was incredibly heavy. The crowd, slightly bewildered, watched for the slightest word, the least flutter of the woman's eyelids, for a sign. But Zahra knew that her young friend would say nothing further.

The mourners resumed their lamentations.

"For the last time, I ask you to speak up: if you have anything to say, now is the time to say it. Afterward, it will be too late."

He waited for a few seconds, then turned to Morteza Ramazani, and, bending deferentially toward him, asked him with the utmost show of respect: "Mr. Ramazani, as the father of the adulteress, do you have anything to say?"

The stooped old man tried to straighten up, then screamed with rage: "Let God's will be done. . . . She is no longer my daughter. . . . I am no longer her father. . . . She is a stranger to me. . . . Let us get this over and done with as soon as possible!"

117

"Long live Mr. Ramazani," several voices rang out. "He's right. Let's get this over and done with as quickly as possible."

Then, turning to Sheik Hassan, who had been silent for some time now, the mayor asked him the same question: "Mr. Lajevardi, as the representative in this village of our most revered imam, do you have anything to add?"

Sheik Hassan shook the sleeves of his cleric's robe, raised high the Koran, around which was wrapped his holy beads, and said: "May the will of the Almighty be done, and may Islamic law be carried out."

The traveling clowns, as though hewn of stone, were staring fixedly at the ceremony unfolding before their eyes. Since they were standing at some distance from the crowd of villagers, they had been forgotten, and no one even thought to look at them.

It was then that everything began.

With a sweeping gesture of both his arms, Machdi Ebrahim motioned for the crowd to move back several steps. He took a piece of cord from his pocket and counted out fifteen cubits. He carefully cut the cord and handed it to Shokrollah.

"This measures somewhere in the neighborhood of twenty-two to twenty-five feet," he said. "Using the hole as your center, go draw me a circle. Mark it with quicklime."

Using Soraya's head as the center, Shokrollah drew a circle on the ground.

The stage was set. The target was visible to all, a motionless black-and-white spot that the participants in this ghoulish game were going to try and hit.

118

The crowd spread out around the circumference of the circle. It was so quiet you could have heard the proverbial pin drop. One would have thought that the village was taking part in some ancestral ritual, the rules of which were familiar to one and all and had been for generations, rules that had been handed down from father to son, with Machdi Ebrahim acting as arbiter.

The traveling clowns were afraid to breathe, wanting to move closer but frightened that if they did, some of the stones might hit them, for they were stationed directly behind the woman, therefore directly in front of the armed villagers. The victim's head was only about forty-five to fifty feet in front of them, and all they could see of her was the cascade of dark hair spread out on the ground around her.

The mayor took a stone and handed it to Soraya's father: "It is to you," he said, "that befalls the honor of throwing the first stone. . . . Please proceed."

The old man set his cane down on the ground and took the large stone in his hand. He gave thanks to God, drew his arm back and, as he threw the stone with all his might in the direction of his daughter, he shouted: "Allah be praised! . . . There, whore, take that!"

He missed the mark. Ebrahim handed him a second stone, and once again, screaming abuse, the old man threw it. Four times he tried to strike his daughter, in vain.

In a state of rage, he said: "Give me another stone. I'm going to crush her skull. . . . I'm going to split open the woman's head!"

Ebrahim made him understand that, no matter what, he could not advance beyond the white line, for that would be in defiance of God's laws.

Then it was Ghorban-Ali's turn. He had rolled up his sleeves and had four rocks neatly piled next to his feet. He waited for the mayor's signal.

"Your turn, my boy," the mayor said to him affectionately, "and may God guide your arm."

The presumably cuckolded husband drew back his arm and then launched his stone, which streaked toward the woman's head, missing by a scant six inches. Soraya remained perfectly still, showing no sign of fear, not even batting an eyelash.

"Good shot, Ghorban-Ali," came the cries from the men in the front rows. "Try again. . . . You'll get her next time, the filthy bitch!"

Soraya's husband picked up a second stone, juggled it for a moment in his hand, as if checking out its size and weight, and glanced around at his public. One would have thought he was an athlete in some stadium trying to break a world record. Once again he reared back, and threw the second stone, which just grazed the woman's head.

There was a collective sigh of disappointment from the spectators, but before they could catch their breath a third stone was thrown, this one striking the victim's right shoulder.

A barely audible sound came from her mouth, and her chest gave a slight shudder.

The crowd was screaming hysterically now, and there were ripples of applause from the men. The shadow of a smile flitted across Ghorban-Ali's face; he picked up another stone, aimed more carefully, and threw it as hard as he could. This time the stone struck the woman on the forehead, just at the hairline. The skin burst open, blood began to trickle down her face, as Soraya's head jerked violently backward.

A shudder of pleasure and joy ran through the crowd. Without realizing it, the villagers had moved several steps forward, crossing the white line that marked the outer boundary of their firing range.

"That's it, you got her! Good for you, Ghorban-Ali. He got her, did you see? Throw another stone, go ahead, give the slut what she deserves!"

The victim's two sons were next. They both picked up stones and threw them at the same time. One of them struck her on the head. There was a sound, like a loud hiccup, as her head again jerked back.

The itinerant troupe, hypnotized by the spectacle and incapable of making the slightest gesture or uttering a single word, did not dare draw any closer. As it was, several of the stones had rolled almost up to where they were standing.

Now the stones were flying thick and fast, piling up on the ground around them. And there, only a few feet in front of them, was a head whose face they never saw, a head that kept bobbing to and fro in time to the stones that were striking it. They had remarked that despite the mayor's dire warning, the villagers had been creeping closer and closer to their target, and as a result there were many more direct hits than when the spectacle began.

Finally it was Sheik Hassan's turn. He put his Koran in his left hand and, with his right, picked up a large stone. But before he threw he turned back to the crowd and said with great bombast: "I am not the one who is throwing this stone. . . . It is God who is guiding my arm. . . . It is he who commands me and the revenge I am meting out is not for me, but for our imam, revenge for the heinous crime this woman has committed."

The applause of the crowd was deafening.

"I shall throw as many stones as it takes to kill this bitch. And afterward the rest of you can throw your stones as well."

As soon as blood had begun to flow, Zahra Khanum had turned away and left. She knew that Soraya's martyrdom was going to last for several minutes before merciful death finally folded her in his arms. The unbearable violence of the scene, which seemed to galvanize the rest of the villagers and turn them into monsters, completely overwhelmed her. She knew them all, every last one of them, had seen most of them born, and suddenly they were nothing but a mass of hate and opprobrium.

Pain and sorrow filled her heart. She sat down on the wooden bench in front of the baker's shop and stared at the ground.

Every time she heard a shout from the crowd, she knew that another stone had struck her niece.

She blamed herself for never even having tried to stop the stoning, although she knew full well that there was nothing she could have done to prevent it. Never in her long life had she felt so ashamed.

Machdi Ebrahim, who held her in high esteem and had often listened to her, had become more and more easily influenced as he grew older, and he had fallen under the spell of this mullah. Soraya's failure to speak out and defend herself, plus her own panic and the lies bruited about by both Soraya's husband and Hashem did the rest.

"If only I had had the courage to say something in defense of that poor child, who is completely innocent," she kept saying to herself over and over again.

Zahra, usually so strong and forceful, had suddenly grown fearful and cowardly, just like all the other women in Kupayeh, completely submissive to the laws made by men.

Would Machdi Ebrahim have listened to her if she had told him everything she knew, everything she had learned, seen, and understood? Would she have been able to bring the man to his senses, he who in times past had so often sought her counsel?

But hadn't he actually taken part in this revolting plot? He who was generally so reserved and fair-minded had in the space of a few months become violent, arrogant, and authoritarian, as if there were something too shameful to mention that he was getting out of this despicable affair.

In the center of the circle, Soraya was slowly expiring. Her head and chest were little more than a shapeless mass of bloody flesh. The noisy crowd, completely out of control, broke ranks and moved in even closer, ready for the kill. Her scalp was nothing more than a gaping wound; her jaw had exploded; her eyes and nose burst open. Her head drooped at a grotesque angle, like some bizarre carnival mask, over what remained of her right shoulder.

In the front row, Hassan, his robe spattered with blood, raised his arm and called for silence. "My dear friends . . . listen to me for a moment. . . . I believe that God has done his work. I believe that his will has been done. Would someone like to check and make certain the harlot is dead?"

Several men raised their hands. Hassan picked Said the well digger. The man lay down on the ground right next to the victim and put his ear close to Soraya's open mouth. "She's still alive. . . . The bitch still hasn't croaked," he said to Sheik Hassan, getting to his feet.

A man slowly stepped forward, holding a stone above his head with both hands, and brought it down directly on top of her skull. Another followed, picked up a brick that was lying there next to the victim, and hit her furiously with it half a dozen times. The skull burst open, and the brains spilled out onto the ground.

At that point an immense cry of joy broke out.

"Allah Akbar! Allah Akbar! God is great! . . . Praise be to God!"

Hassan Lajevardi raised his Koran in a sign of victory and commanded the villagers to form a circle around him. "Let us give thanks to God, the All-powerful."

A sudden silence came over the assembly. Then, after a brief moment of meditation, the crowd intoned, together with the mullah: "In the Name of God, the Compassionate, the Merciful."

Before the circle had been formed, the men had been standing in a tight knot around Soraya, hiding from the itinerant players the sight that was now in plain view: a bloody mass around which a horde of insects had already begun to swarm. Horrified, they took a few steps back but were unable to tear their eyes from that hellish vision. A dog was pacing back and forth around the broken body but seemed afraid to move in closer.

Seated there on her bench, in a state of complete exhaustion and despair, Zahra Khanum heard nothing further. She knew that it was over and that the "law," such as men had willed it, had been carried out.

She did not lift her head when she saw the well-worn guivehs of Machdi Ebrahim stop right next to where she was sitting. The old man cleared his throat and said: "Zahra, it's all over. . . . Justice has been done. . . . Now everything is all right." He paused, then went on: "Don't you have anything to say to me?"

Only then did she straighten up, look directly at the man who for more than half a century had been her friend, and say: "My poor Ebrahim. . . . All I can feel for you is shame. . . . May Almighty God forgive you for what you have done."

The kadkhoda bid her farewell and walked slowly away, leaning on his cane. From the back, Zahra noted that he was even more stooped than usual.

She felt not even a shred of pity for the man.

8

THE SUN HAD DISAPPEARED behind the trees. Three stray dogs, drawn by the smell of blood, were sniffing nervously about the corpse. The villagers had gone back to their work. As the law required, the body of the martyred woman would remain exposed, as an example to all.

Moving in concentric circles, each one shorter than the last, the dogs edged in closer to the corpse. Then, all of a sudden, one of the dogs dashed forward, tried to seize Soraya's head, and pulled as hard as it could, trying to separate it from the body. Zahra leaped from the bench where she was sitting and ran, stick in hand, screaming like one of the furies: "Get out of there, you filthy beasts; be gone with you!"

She picked up a stone and threw it at the dog, but it missed its mark. The dog backed up a few steps, growled, and bared its fangs. Other villagers arrived on the scene to help chase away the dogs, which took refuge among the members of the itinerant troupe, where they sat licking their paws and growling.

"Bring me a blanket," the old woman said. "And be quick about it. Or a sheet. Anything."

They covered up the remains of the woman who had been stoned to death, then everyone went back to their chores or work. It was about six in the evening. A kind of torpor had settled over the village. At the market, there were few buyers, and the ones that were there spoke in hushed tones. From time to time you could hear the high-pitched cry of a child, a mother's voice calling to her little boy or girl to come home, the cawing of a crow. And, once again, you could hear the sound of the babbling brook and the whisper of the evening breeze in the branches of the trees. The itinerant clowns, still in a state of shock, had begun to unpack their equipment, but they went about it very slowly, as though their hearts weren't in it. They set up their ladder, unrolled their carpet onto the ground, placed one of their monkeys up on a box, and checked their makeup.

Meanwhile, the municipal council had gathered in Sheik Hassan's house to drink tea and smoke. For a long moment they sat there in silence, as if the full weight of what they had just done had finally sunk in. Impassive, Hassan was looking at them from behind his dark glasses, studying each of them in turn. When he had finished his tea, he started to speak.

"Your Honor the Mayor, Mr. Ramazani, my dear Ghorban-Ali, and all of you gathered here, it was necessary for us to have these few moments of reflection and meditation in order to put today's events behind us and move on. God wanted us to take these few quiet moments. Nor should we forget that all we have done was to carry out his will. Remember that this woman was not the first woman to be stoned to death in our country since the law of the Almighty has been reinstated here. Dozens of others before her have met a like fate, and others will follow if, once again, God is desecrated or defiled. . . . We have nothing to fear from our act. Tomorrow, as early as possible, I shall inform the authorities of what happened here today. Let me repeat: in the space of a few short hours, Kupayeh has become an exemplary village, one that will be talked about throughout the land."

The dozen or so men who were sitting there listened earnestly to Hassan's words, which were interrupted only by the slurping sound they made as they drank their tea and their murmurs of approval as they nodded in agreement with everything he was saying.

"My friends, evil was abroad in this village and we were unaware of it. . . . Fortunately, the All-powerful, in his infinite mercy, led me forth into these mountains. God willed that I save your village from evil and from sin. Let us give thanks to God and to his Prophet. . . ."

And together they prayed aloud: "In the Name of God, the Compassionate, the Merciful."

All of a sudden Morteza Ramazani was wracked by sobs. With both fists he pounded himself on the head, moaning and wailing between sobs: "I am ashamed. . . . Oh my God, I am overcome with shame. . . . But how is this possible? Oh God Almighty, have pity on me. . . . My brethren, forgive me."

The other men in the room shifted uneasily, not quite sure how to react or respond. The mullah, sensing their uneasiness, moved quickly to keep matters from getting out of hand.

"Mr. Ramazani, there is no reason for you to be ashamed. . . . We love and respect you. You are the eldest among us, and you should know that you can always count on our love and affection if ever you should

128

have need of them. This village is your home, and our doors will always be open to you. We shall never forget that it was you who cast the first stone at the adulteress, it was you who showed us the way, provided us with the example, and we followed you as a son follows the father. For that we shall always be grateful."

Sheik Hassan's words were greeted by a round of hearty applause.

The old man mumbled a few words of thanks to Sheik Hassan, then remained prostrate, his face buried in his hands.

At this point Machdi Ebrahim began to speak: "Who would have thought, when we got up this morning, that such dire things would have come to pass in this village today? It was God's will, and as Mr. Lajevardi has just reminded us, all we did was apply his law. But it will doubtless take us a long time to forget what has happened here today — "

"That's not so," interrupted Ghorban-Ali, who was seated at some distance from the rest of the group. "That's not true at all. As for me, I've already forgotten everything. . . . I don't even want to think about it again. I don't ever want to talk about it again. As far as I'm concerned, it's over and done with!"

And with that he got to his feet, knocked over a chair, and strode across the room, muttering to himself. Then he slammed the door behind him.

Again, a heavy silence fell over the room. Machdi Ebrahim eventually took up where he had left off: "Let me repeat what I've already said: it will take us a long time to forget what has happened here today, especially us older people. Whenever God manifests

129

himself, it is a lesson for us all, old and young alike. It is not only Morteza who is suffering. We are all suffering as well."

Sheik Hassan nodded in approval.

"Now we come to the matter of Soraya's burial, and I think that Mr. Lajevardi has some thoughts on the subject, do you not?"

Everyone looked at the mullah, who had not anticipated the question.

"Yes . . . uh . . . yes, I do have some rather strong thoughts on the subject. The woman's body must be removed from where it is before the sun goes down. But I think — and I'm sure you agree with me — that she should not be buried in our cemetery. That is not the rightful place for her to be interred."

This time it was Ebrahim's turn to be taken aback. The rest of the group were of Hassan's opinion.

"We do not want her to be buried in the cemetery," echoed Shokrollah, as if the idea were his own. "It is not right that her final resting place be among our dead."

"I agree," said Mohammad Ghorbani, "not among our dead."

"We don't want her there," a third man agreed.

At that point Ebrahim turned to Morteza and asked his opinion.

"And what do you think, my friend?"

The old man seemed not to hear.

"Morteza, what is your wish? Where do you want Soraya to be buried?"

The father of the woman who had been stoned to death remained prostrate and silent.

"If everyone agrees that she should not be buried in the cemetery," said Sheik Hassan, "then you must decide where outside the village she should be buried. You know the region better than I. I leave it to you to decide."

The men began discussing the question among themselves, but no one could agree. Their discussions were endless, and for a moment one had the impression they might even come to blows. At this point the mullah intervened: "If I understand you all correctly, you don't want her to be buried in the cemetery but you also don't want her buried in the fields outside, for those fields belong to you and you don't want them desecrated. . . . Am I correct? Is that what you are arguing about?"

The men all nodded, ever so slightly.

"I think I have a solution, but first I want your unanimous agreement. You all agree that Soraya Manutchehri has defiled and humiliated us?"

"Yes," they responded in unison. "She has defiled and humiliated us all."

"You all agree that she was not a good Muslim and that she lied to God?"

Once again the assembly indicated its assent.

"Do you also agree that she turned away from the words of the Prophet?"

Again they shouted that, yes, they did agree.

"And that she betrayed the instructions of our beloved imam?"

"Yes, she betrayed them!"

"So, I say to you, my proposition is the following: she will not be buried at all."

Dumbfounded, the group looked at one another in silence.

"You heard me: she will not be buried."

There was a brief silence, then Machdi Ebrahim broke in: "We have listened to your words, Sheik Hassan, and I am sure your decision is a wise one."

"Soraya Manutchehri led a life of deceit and dishonor. She betrayed the confidence God had placed in her, as she betrayed the confidence of the Prophet and of our imam. She lied to her family, her husband, and her children. She betrayed the entire village, and she tried to lead our friend Hashem, who still mourns the untimely death of his wife, from the path of righteousness. She lived like a harlot. She died like a harlot. Her body will therefore be thrown into the fields, there to be devoured by the beasts whose role it will be to see that her remains disappear."

Ebrahim could not believe what he was hearing. He would have liked to say something, but before he could all the others had already heartily approved the imam's words.

"That sounds like a good decision to us. . . . Let the bitch return to the animals where she belongs. . . . No burial. Only proper Muslims deserve a proper burial."

Hassan Lajevardi raised both his hands.

"My dear friends, I suggest that we men, who live here in dignity, absolve ourselves from this task. Let the women take care of it. If Said or Rassoul want to help disinter the corpse with their picks and shovels, so be it, but afterward it's up to the women to rid us of this defiled corpse."

"Well said," the men said. "Let's get started."

132

They all rose and left the house. Hassan and Ebrahim began walking more quickly. As they went, the mullah leaned over to the mayor and said to him: "I think you should go over to Zahra Khanum and let her know about this immediately. You're the only one who can make her understand our decision. And the women won't make a move without her agreement."

"That's not going to be easy," Ebrahim growled. "You know the woman."

"Not as well as you do. . . . You'll find the necessary words. But don't waste any time."

The sound of a trumpet and drum rang out. Everyone looked over in the direction of the strolling performers. The goat was halfway up the stepladder, and the monkey was busily turning somersaults.

"Stop that!" screamed Hassan as he hastened over toward the clowns. "Stop what you're doing this instant. This is not the time. Wait until the square has been cleared; then you can begin."

The music stopped, and the monkey stopped doing its tricks.

The kadkhoda had gone over to Zahra's house and knocked on her door. He was not looking forward to the encounter, and he had rehearsed in his mind exactly what he was going to say. He had not been swayed from his duties during the entire day, and now that the stoning had come to pass, now that it was all over, he was not about to yield. He knocked again. At last he heard a voice answer; he opened the door and went in.

"May Almighty God be with you, Zahra Khanum, and with all your family."

She returned his greeting with a mere nod of ac-

133

knowledgment, and invited him to sit down. The old woman, seated on the same cushions on the floor where Soraya had sat only a few hours earlier, was puffing on a cigarette that she had just rolled for herself. A steaming cup of tea was in front of her, but contrary to custom she did not offer any to her visitor.

"I know why you have come, and the answer is no."

Disconcerted by her words, the mayor said: "You're saying no to me about what? I haven't even told you what I'm here for."

"I know very well what brought you here: poor Soraya's burial. I want nothing to do with it. You're the ones who have committed this monstrosity, so you take care of it. We women won't lift a finger to help."

Not a very good start, Ebrahim said to himself. He took his pipe from his pocket and meticulously filled it with tobacco.

"That's not what I came here to talk about," he said. "At least not entirely."

He knew he had better take things in hand again, or the old woman would throw him out of her house before he had even informed her of Sheik Hassan's plan.

"Zahra Khanum, I have come to inform you of the decision made by the town council."

"You mean you've come here to tell about the decisions made by that bird of misfortune who wears the garb of a cleric. Let me tell you something, for you and I are very old friends. I know that in your heart of hearts you don't agree with what you've been sent here to tell me, and I also know that I won't agree with it either. Tell me if I'm wrong."

The mayor knew that this task was going to be even

harder than he had thought, but he refrained from interrupting her. "What I think is not important. We voted, and the decision was made. I have to see that it is carried out."

"So why come to tell me about it? Do women have any say in this village now? Have they had any say for the past several years?"

"I've come to tell you that Soraya's burial has posed a problem. No one wants her to be buried in the village cemetery."

"Have you asked my opinion? And what if I were to tell you that I would like her to be buried with my family, next to her mother?"

"That's not really what I came to tell you. Sheik Hassan is of the opinion that she shouldn't be buried at all."

"Say that to me again, Machdi Ebrahim! Do you dare tell me one more time what you have just said? She doesn't deserve to be buried *at all?*"

"According to God's law, no woman who has been stoned to death has the right to interment. That's what Sheik Hassan says."

"And how does he know? . . . Perhaps he has already stoned other women to death, is that how?"

"He says that those who have strayed from God's path have no right to be buried with those who have lived with dignity."

The discussion between the two old friends was long and bitter. They both refused to budge from their positions, but by the time the mayor emerged from Zahra's house he had got what he wanted. At nightfall, the women of the village would take Soraya's body outside the village limits.

Said and Rassoul had the macabre task of disinterring the body. Despite the canvas cover that had been thrown over the woman who had been stoned to death, flies were already swarming. The two men wielded their picks and shovels. The odor was unbearable. The dogs that had drawn near were barking more and more fiercely.

When Soraya's torso was freed from its prison of dirt, the head fell to one side, like some watermelon that had exploded, and with a snapping noise like the sound of a branch breaking, separated itself from the body. Both men stopped in their tracks and turned their heads away.

When the ditch was large and deep enough, both men stepped down into it and took the now decapitated body, still clothed in Zahra's white dress, and lifted it out of the pit.

Sheik Hassan, who had been watching, spoke up: "Thank you, gentlemen; now go get cleaned up. God will reward you for what you have done."

Said and Rassoul hurried off in the direction of the stream.

"Cover the body for a few moments, before the women arrive to take over."

The dogs, who were in a state of frenzy, had approached the corpse, and one of them seized the piece of canvas between his teeth and pulled it off, once again exposing the mutilated body for all to see. Only when the women arrived did the dogs, made ravenous by the smell, beat a hasty retreat.

Zahra was sick to her stomach when she saw the unbearable spectacle at close range. She covered her nose with a handkerchief and issued some curt instructions. A large sheet was spread out on the ground, and with the help of Akram and Sakineh, she carried Soraya's body over and laid it in the winding sheet. A blanket was brought over, in which they wrapped the body. Then they lifted it onto a cart, which the women pulled with considerable difficulty across and beyond the village square, followed in close pursuit by the dogs, who appeared more and more threatening.

Machdi Ebrahim had appointed three men to clean up the area where the execution had taken place. The hole was filled in, the ground flattened out and raked to remove any trace of blood. Then Said brought in a wheelbarrow full of fresh soil, which was scattered over the spot.

By now night had fallen, and with it came a welcoming breeze that cooled things down. In the middle of the square, the itinerant performers had once again set up their equipment.

Meanwhile, about half a mile downstream from the village, the women paused to catch their breath. Zahra appeared utterly exhausted. In the space of a single day she had aged more than she had in the past twenty years. She looked even more shrunken than before. Yesterday evening, she had embraced Soraya, who had come by to bring Zahra some fruit from her garden. And now, only twenty-four hours later, here she was transporting her niece's martyred body.

She was living a nightmare.

"How far are we taking her, Zahra Khanum?" asked one of the women, breaking the silence. She was still holding tightly onto the cart, which tended to slip and slide on the arid soil.

"Just one more turn in the road," Zahra said. "We'll take Soraya down near the stream. It is a spot she loved. I think it's the best place to take her."

Her companions accepted her suggestion and painfully continued their funereal procession. The dogs still followed some distance behind, sniffing as they went.

Finally the procession came to a halt. They wedged the cart's wheels with two large stones, to keep it from moving. The women knotted their chadors around their waists, then, with infinite caution, took hold of the body wrapped in its rough, brown blanket. They carried it about thirty feet or so, down away from the road, and deposited it near the rapids, between two thorny bushes.

Zahra made sure that Soraya's body was fully covered, and that the corners of the blanket were all securely tucked in, so that no insects could get in. She surrounded the body with a ring of large stones, then covered it with branches and dead leaves. The women remained there in total silence for a long time. Then they climbed back up the slope and returned to the village, dragging behind them the empty, bloodstained cart. The nearer they got to the village, the louder the sound of the trumpet and drum became.

A hallucinatory spectacle greeted Zahra when she reached the square. On the exact same spot where Soraya had been stoned to death, a joyful fire was now burning, and around its flames the villagers were dancing. The strolling performers had started their show.

The village women had donned their finest multicolored dresses and were turning in circles, while the men, white handkerchiefs in hand, danced around one another, short cries of joy emanating from their mouths. Zahra, rooted to the spot as though she had turned to stone, could not believe her eyes. Only a few hours after the execution, these people were letting off steam, singing and dancing as if it were a *chahar shambeh souri*, when the whole country lighted fires of joy to exorcise ancient demons.

She recognized both Said and Rassoul, who had just disinterred the woman's body; Mehdi the butcher, who was cavorting around Massoud the barber. Farther on, she saw Ebrahim's two deputies, both of whom were singing and dancing; then there was the one-eyed man, and Yadolah the shepherd and his son, both of whom were laughing heartily; and there were Karim, Asghar, Majid, and Moshen, Rahmatollah and Ali-Akbar, and all the others. Standing a little apart from the others, Hussein-Ali and Hassan-Ali were busily devouring a watermelon.

Finally her eyes found Machdi Ebrahim and Sheik Hassan, who were standing in front of the baker's shop. Next to them, all shriveled up, was Morteza, who looked as though he was half asleep. The two men were in deep discussion. As soon as they saw the women walking toward them, they broke off their conversation and greeted them with a slight nod of the head. Zahra walked by them without so much as a glance in their direction.

She went into her house and slammed the door. The

other women disappeared into the night, leaving the
village to its obscene celebration.

Very early the next morning, Zahra emerged from her
house, and, hugging the walls so as not to be noticed,
she slipped out of the village like a thief.

The ashes of the previous night's fire were still smok-
ing. The itinerant performers were sleeping next to
their vehicles. She followed the same path she had taken
the previous evening for a good half mile, until she
reached the sixth curve. There she cut through the
woods, and, approaching the stream, she could not repress a cry of horror.

Barely three steps in front of her, four stray dogs
were fast asleep, gorged from their collective meal,
their snouts and their fur covered with dried blood.
Nothing remained of the poor woman's body. They had
devoured everything. Here and there were scattered
human bones, the vestige of the brown blanket, and a
shred or two of her clothing; a little farther off lay what
remained of Soraya's head. . . .

The old woman leaned against a tree and threw up.
Then she sat down on her haunches. Her strength had
deserted her. For an hour she remained there, unable
to move. Finally some of her energy returned; she got
to her feet, and with all the strength she could muster,
she picked up the biggest rock around and threw it as
hard as she could at one of the sleeping dogs. The animal
howled with pain and beat a quick retreat in the under-
brush, followed by the other frightened animals.

Once again Zahra Khanum tied her chador around her

140

waist, kneeled down, and began to scratch the earth with her hands. The ground was soft and moist. When the hole was large enough, she gathered, one by one, her niece Soraya's bones, took them down and washed them in the stream, then returned and carefully placed them in the earthen grave, which she covered over with leaves and branches. Then, and only then, did she pray and burst into tears.

Glossary

Arbab	In general, a large landowner or a wealthy businessman.
Ayatollah	A high-ranking dignitary of the Shiite clergy.
Baksheesh	A payment, as either a tip or a bribe, to gain some advantage or expedite a particular service.
Chador	The veil that women wear.
Chahar shambeh souri	A popular Iranian holiday when people build a fire, make themselves up, and dance.
Guivehs	Espadrilles, a kind of flat sandal with a hemp sole.
Hamman	A Turkish steam bath
Kadkhoda	The person in charge of a village, named by his fellow villagers, whose role is roughly that of a mayor. He generally reports to the authorities of a larger, neighboring town or city.
Khanum	A title comparable to lady or Mrs.

Khorsi	A low, heated table, around which family members gather during the long winter evenings.
Machdi	The title given to someone who has made the pilgrimage to the holy city of Machad.
Mahkum	Guilty
Mullah	A Muslim of the quasi-clerical class trained in traditional law and doctrine.
Nowruz	Iranian New Year (March 21).
Pahlavi	A monetary unit of Iran, still current today, worth a hundred rials.
Rial	A unit of Iranian currency.
Samovar	A kind of teapot that, in Iran, is always kept full of boiling water so that tea can be served at a moment's notice.
Salam al leikum	Good morning; hello.
Sang sâr	Stoning.
Savaki	A former functionary of the royal political police, equivalent to a torturer.
Seyed	A member of the clergy who is descended from the Prophet and is thereby entitled to wear the black turban.
Sharbat	Syrup.
Sigheh	An official concubine authorized by Islam.

Sizda bedar   The thirteenth day after *Nowruz* when, according to Persian tradition, people must leave their houses so the site can be cleansed of demons. In general, entire towns and cities decamp to the countryside for this day.

Tasbi   Prayer box.